Introduction to Representation

For information on the PreK–2 grades and 6–8 grades series, see the Heinemann
website, www.heinemann.com.

Introduction to Representation
Grades 3–5

Bonnie H. Ennis
Kimberly S. Witeck

The Math Process Standards Series
Susan O'Connell, Series Editor

HEINEMANN
Portsmouth, NH

Heinemann
A division of Reed Elsevier Inc.
361 Hanover Street
Portsmouth, NH 03801–3912
www.heinemann.com

Offices and agents throughout the world

The authors and publisher wish to thank those who have generously given permission to reprint borrowed material:

Excerpts from *Principles and Standards for School Mathematics*. Copyright © 2000 by the National Council of Teachers of Mathematics. Reprinted with permission. All rights reserved.

Library of Congress Cataloging-in-Publication Data
Ennis, Bonnie.
    Introduction to representation : grades 3–5 / Bonnie Ennis, Kimberly Witeck.
        p. cm.—(The math process standards series)
    Includes bibliographical references.
    ISBN-13: 978-0-325-01104-2
    ISBN-10: 0-325-01104-4
    1. Mathematics—Study and teaching (Elementary).   I. Witeck, Kimberly.
II. Title.   III. Series.
    QA135.6.W58   2007
    372.7'2—dc22   2006030055

Editor: Emily Michie Birch
Production: Elizabeth Valway
Cover design: Night & Day Design
Composition: Publishers' Design and Production Services, Inc.
CD production: Nicole Russell and Marla Berry
Manufacturing: Jamie Carter

Printed in the United States of America on acid-free paper
11   10   09   08   07   ML   1   2   3   4   5

On the CD-ROM

In order to be effective mathematicians, students need to develop understanding of critical math content. They need to understand number and operations, algebra, measurement, geometry, and data analysis and probability. Through continued study of these content domains, students gain a comprehensive understanding of mathematics as a subject with varied and interconnected concepts. As math teachers, we attempt to provide students with exposure to, exploration in, and reflection about the many skills and concepts that make up the study of mathematics.

Even with a deep understanding of math content, however, students may lack important skills that can assist them in their development as effective mathematicians. Along with content knowledge, students need an understanding of the processes used by mathematicians. They must learn to problem solve, communicate their ideas, reason through math situations, prove their conjectures, make connections between and among math concepts, and represent their mathematical thinking. Development of content alone does not provide students with the means to explore, express, or apply that content. As we strive to develop effective mathematicians, we are challenged to develop both students' content understanding and process skills.

The National Council of Teachers of Mathematics (2000) has outlined critical content and process standards in its *Principles and Standards for School Mathematics* document. These standards have become the road map for the development of textbooks, curriculum materials, and student assessments. These standards have provided a framework for thinking about what needs to be taught in math classrooms and how various skills and concepts can be blended together to create a seamless math curriculum. The first five standards outline content standards and expectations related to number and operations, algebra, geometry, measurement, and data analysis and probability. The second five standards outline the process goals of problem solving, reasoning and proof, communication, connections, and representations. A strong understanding of these standards empowers teachers to identify and select activities within their curricula to produce powerful learning. The standards provide a vision for what teachers hope their students will achieve.

This book is a part of a vital series designed to assist teachers in understanding the NCTM Process Standards and the ways in which they impact and guide student learning. An additional goal of this series is to provide practical ideas to support teachers as they ensure that the acquisition of process skills has a critical place in their math instruction. Through this series, teachers will gain an understanding of each process standard as well as gather ideas for bringing that standard to life within their math classrooms. It offers practical ideas for lesson development, implementation, and assessment that work with any curriculum. Each book in the series focuses on a critical process skill in a highlighted grade band and all books are designed to encourage reflection about teaching and learning. The series also highlights the interconnected nature of the process and content standards by showing correlations between them and showcasing activities that address multiple standards.

Students who develop an understanding of content skills and cultivate the process skills that allow them to apply that content understanding become effective mathematicians. Our goal as teachers is to support and guide students as they develop both their content knowledge and their process skills, so they are able to continue to expand and refine their understanding of mathematics. This series is a guide for math educators who aspire to teach students more than math content. It is a guide to assist teachers in understanding and teaching the critical processes through which students learn and make sense of mathematics.

Susan O'Connell
Series Editor

We would like to thank many people for their support, expertise, guidance, and encouragement during this project. First, thank you to Sue O'Connell for encouraging us to take on this project; for your patient support in reading our work; and for helping to give us a jump start when we needed it. And to Emily Birch, Executive Editor for Math and Science at Heinemann, thanks for always being available to give feedback, support, and encouragement.

From Bonnie Ennis

To the students, teachers, and administrators of the Wicomico County Public Schools, thank you for your advice, support, and expertise throughout the years. A special thank-you to the math professional development coaches of Wicomico County, who continue to amaze me on a daily basis with their creativity, enthusiasm, and willingness to do everything we ask in support of the teachers of our district. It is a pleasure to work with such wonderful professionals.

To Kelly, Jordon, and Taylor, thanks for taking time to do math at the pool, and to Mrs. Young's summer school class, thank you for reminding me how wonderful it is to be a teacher.

To my husband, David, and our two sons, Brian and Bruce, thank you for your continued support and words of encouragement, and finally, to my mother, thank you for being my first teacher.

From Kimberly Witeck

To the community of teachers and students at Braddock Elementary in Annandale, Virginia, thank you for providing invaluable feedback, support, and your expertise. Thanks especially to Cynthia Botzin, principal at Braddock, for being a model leader for all in the field of education and for allowing me to work with students at the school to gather data and work samples for the book; Beth Rodriguez and Judy Hall, Title I math teachers and coaches, for their expertise, feedback on particular chapters, and moral support; Gwenanne Salkind, Title I Assistant Program Supervisor, for her expertise and guidance in clarifying concepts in the book; and Shannon Butler, Aaron Davis, Christine Fisher, Katie Fowle, Johanna Lozier, and Courtney Sommers, teachers at Braddock, for allowing me to work with their students.

The following students were a pleasure to work with and contributed work samples or allowed their photographs to be included in the book: Leandro Becerra, Rebecca Benedetto, Nora Benedetto, Elizabeth Benedetto, Sarah Hobbs, Trace Mondell, Rebecca Namm, Kelsey Pendergast, Alvaro Perez, Annie Pham, Ana Rivas, Christina Uglietta, and Tommy Virnston.

Some other people also provided welcome support: our friend and baby-sitter, Yodit Gebretsadik, enabled me to devote the time necessary to finish this project. My sister, Christine Slaughter, lent her editing expertise and gave words of encouragement.

Finally, I could not have completed this project without the unwavering support of my husband, Chris, my parents, Skip and Jackie Sterling, who always believed I could finish this project, and my beautiful children, Aidan and Caroline. I love you.

Problem-Solving Standard

Instructional programs from prekindergarten through grade 12 should enable all students to—

- build new mathematical knowledge through problem solving;

- solve problems that arise in mathematics and in other contexts;

- apply and adapt a variety of appropriate strategies to solve problems;

- monitor and reflect on the process of mathematical problem solving.

Reasoning and Proof Standard

Instructional programs from prekindergarten through grade 12 should enable all students to—

- recognize reasoning and proof as fundamental aspects of mathematics;

- make and investigate mathematical conjectures;

- develop and evaluate mathematical arguments and proofs;

- select and use various types of reasoning and methods of proof.

---

* Standards are listed with the permission of the National Council of Teachers of Mathematics (NCTM). NCTM does not endorse the content or validity of these alignments.

Communication Standard

Instructional programs from prekindergarten through grade 12 should enable all students to—

- organize and consolidate their mathematical thinking through communication;

- communicate their mathematical thinking coherently and clearly to peers, teachers, and others;

- analyze and evaluate the mathematical thinking and strategies of others;

- use the language of mathematics to express mathematical ideas precisely.

Connections Standards

Instructional programs from prekindergarten through grade 12 should enable all students to—

- recognize and use connections among mathematical ideas;

- understand how mathematical ideas interconnect and build on one another to produce a coherent whole;

- recognize and apply mathematics in contexts outside of mathematics.

Representation Standard

Instructional programs from prekindergarten through grade 12 should enable all students to—

- create and use representations to organize, record, and communicate mathematical ideas;

- select, apply, and translate among mathematical representations to solve problems;

- use representations to model and interpret physical, social, and mathematical phenomena.

NCTM Content Standards and Expectations for Grades 3–5

NUMBER AND OPERATIONS

	Expectations
Instructional programs from prekindergarten through grade 12 should enable all students to—	**In grades 3–5 all students should—**
understand numbers, ways of representing numbers, relationships among numbers, and number systems	• understand the place-value structure of the base ten number system and be able to represent and compare whole numbers and decimals; • recognize equivalent representations for the same number and generate them by decomposing and composing numbers; • develop understanding of fractions as parts of unit wholes, as parts of a collection, as locations on number lines, and as divisions of whole numbers; • use models, benchmarks, and equivalent forms to judge the size of fractions; • recognize and generate equivalent forms of commonly used fractions, decimals, and percents; • explore numbers less than 0 by extending the number line and through familiar applications; • describe classes of numbers according to characteristics such as the nature of their factors.
understand meanings of operations and how they relate to one another	• understand various meanings of multiplication and division; • understand the effects of multiplying and dividing whole numbers; • identify and use relationships between operations, such as division as the inverse of multiplication, to solve problems; • understand and use properties of operations, such as the distributivity of multiplication over addition.

	Expectations
Instructional programs from prekindergarten through grade 12 should enable all students to—	**In grades 3–5 all students should—**
compute fluently and make reasonable estimates	• develop fluency with basic number combinations for multiplication and division and use these combinations to mentally compute related problems, such as 30×50; • develop fluency in adding, subtracting, multiplying, and dividing whole numbers; • develop and use strategies to estimate the results of whole-number computations and to judge the reasonableness of such results; • develop and use strategies to estimate computations involving fractions and decimals in situations relevant to students' experience; • use visual models, benchmarks, and equivalent forms to add and subtract commonly used fractions and decimals; • select appropriate methods and tools for computing with whole numbers from among mental computation, estimation, calculators, and paper and pencil according to the context and nature of the computation and use the selected method or tools.

ALGEBRA

	Expectations
Instructional programs from prekindergarten through grade 12 should enable all students to—	**In grades 3–5 all students should—**
understand patterns, relations, and functions	• describe, extend, and make generalizations about geometric and numeric patterns; • represent and analyze patterns and functions, using words, tables, and graphs.

	Expectations
Instructional programs from prekindergarten through grade 12 should enable all students to—	**In grades 3–5 all students should—**
represent and analyze mathematical situations and structures using algebraic symbols	• identify such properties as commutativity, associativity, and distributivity and use them to compute with whole numbers; • represent the idea of a variable as an unknown quantity using a letter or a symbol; • express mathematical relationships using equations.
use mathematical models to represent and understand quantitative relationships	• model problem situations with objects and use representations such as graphs, tables, and equations to draw conclusions.
analyze change in various contexts	• investigate how a change in one variable relates to a change in a second variable; • identify and describe situations with constant or varying rates of change and compare them.

GEOMETRY

	Expectations
Instructional programs from prekindergarten through grade 12 should enable all students to—	**In grades 3–5 all students should—**
analyze characteristics and properties of two- and three-dimensional geometric shapes and develop mathematical arguments about geometric relationships	• identify, compare, and analyze attributes of two- and three-dimensional shapes and develop vocabulary to describe the attributes; • classify two- and three-dimensional shapes according to their properties and develop definitions of classes of shapes such as triangles and pyramids; • investigate, describe, and reason about the results of subdividing, combining, and transforming shapes; • explore congruence and similarity;

	Expectations
Instructional programs from prekindergarten through grade 12 should enable all students to—	**In grades 3–5 all students should—**
specify locations and describe spatial relationships using coordinate geometry and other representational systems	• make and test conjectures about geometric properties and relationships and develop logical arguments to justify conclusions. • describe location and movement using common language and geometric vocabulary; • make and use coordinate systems to specify locations and to describe paths; • find the distance between points along horizontal and vertical lines of a coordinate system.
apply transformations and use symmetry to analyze mathematical situations	• predict and describe the results of sliding, flipping, and turning two-dimensional shapes; • describe a motion or a series of motions that will show that two shapes are congruent; • identify and describe line and rotational symmetry in two- and three-dimensional shapes and designs.
use visualization, spatial reasoning, and geometric modeling to solve problems	• build and draw geometric objects; • create and describe mental images of objects, patterns, and paths; • identify and build a three-dimensional object from two-dimensional representations of that object; • identify and draw a two-dimensional representation of a three-dimensional object; • use geometric models to solve problems in other areas of mathematics, such as number and measurement; • recognize geometric ideas and relationships and apply them to other disciplines and to problems that arise in the classroom or in everyday life.

	Expectations
Instructional programs from prekindergarten through grade 12 should enable all students to—	**In grades 3–5 all students should—**
understand measurable attributes of objects and the units, systems, and processes of measurement	• understand such attributes as length, area, weight, volume, and size of angle and select the appropriate type of unit for measuring each attribute; • understand the need for measuring with standard units and become familiar with standard units in the customary and metric systems; • carry out simple unit conversions, such as from centimeters to meters, within a system of measurement; • understand that measurements are approximations and how differences in units affect precision; • explore what happens to measurements of a two-dimensional shape such as its perimeter and area when the shape is changed in some way.
apply appropriate techniques, tools, and formulas to determine measurements	• develop strategies for estimating the perimeters, areas, and volumes of irregular shapes; • select and apply appropriate standard units and tools to measure length, area, volume, weight, time, temperature, and the size of angles; • select and use benchmarks to estimate measurements; • develop, understand, and use formulas to find the area of rectangles and related triangles and parallelograms; • develop strategies to determine the surface areas and volumes of rectangular solids.

	Expectations
Instructional programs from prekindergarten through grade 12 should enable all students to—	**In grades 3–5 all students should—**
formulate questions that can be addressed with data and collect, organize, and display relevant data to answer them	• design investigations to address a question and consider how data-collection methods affect the nature of the data set; • collect data using observations, surveys, and experiments; • represent data using tables and graphs such as line plots, bar graphs, and line graphs; • recognize the differences in representing categorical and numerical data.
select and use appropriate statistical methods to analyze data	• describe the shape and important features of a set of data and compare related data sets, with an emphasis on how the data are distributed; • use measures of center, focusing on the median, and understand what each does and does not indicate about the data set; • compare different representations of the same data and evaluate how well each representation shows important aspects of the data.
develop and evaluate inferences and predictions that are based on data	• propose and justify conclusions and predictions that are based on data and design studies to further investigate the conclusions or predictions.
understand and apply basic concepts of probability	• describe events as likely or unlikely and discuss the degree of likelihood using such words as *certain, equally likely,* and *impossible;* • predict the probability of outcomes of simple experiments and test the predictions; • understand that the measure of the likelihood of an event can be represented by a number from 0 to 1.

The Representation Standard

The ways in which mathematical ideas are represented is fundamental to how people can understand and use those ideas.

—National Council of Teachers of Mathematics,
Principles and Standards for School Mathematics

What Are Representations?

What do we teachers mean when we ask students to show their work? Are we asking them to show the numeric computations and steps they took in reaching a solution to a division problem? Are we looking for the right steps in solving an equation? Are we asking them to somehow put on paper the processes and thinking they went through as they developed a solution to a multistep problem? What does it truly mean to ask students to represent their mathematical thinking, and how can we support, model for, and encourage students to put on paper their interpretations of the mathematical models that helped them make those crucial connections between the concrete and the abstract? Representing their solutions is one of the means by which students can communicate to others their mathematical thinking and at the same time clarify in their own mind what meaning lies in the mathematics. While manipulatives provide students with an opportunity to model the mathematics at hand, they are just that: models. It is up to the teacher to help students make the connections between the models and the mathematics. Only by making that connection will students truly understand and internalize the math. Once that connection has been made, students can represent their thinking in words, pictures or symbols, and diagrams and apply their knowledge to more complex problem-solving situations. Representations take many forms: an algorithm that represents a problem situation, a graph that represents data collected in the classroom, an array that shows a multiplication process, or a diagram that illustrates area or perimeter. Numbers, pictures, diagrams, equations, graphs, and models are all forms of mathematical representations. While in the past, standard representations were simply taught to students, teachers are now recognizing the power of alternative representations as tools through which students can explore and enhance their mathematical thinking.

The National Council of Teachers of Mathematics' *Principles and Standards for School Mathematics* (2000) describes representations as fundamental to understanding and applying mathematics, and it makes three recommendations for using them in the mathematics classroom:

1. teachers should employ "representations to model and interpret physical, social, and mathematical phenomena" (NCTM 2000, 70);

2. students should be familiar with and comprehend various representations that can be used to describe phenomena; and

3. students should use mathematical representations to organize their thinking and reflect on numerical or geometric information.

Representations, instead of being taught to students, are valuable ways in which students can explore their own math thinking. Finding ways to represent their ideas pushes students to think more deeply about those ideas as they determine ways to communicate them to others. Providing students with a way of working through their thought processes, representations give us insight into our students' understandings. When students use base ten blocks to model multiplication problems, draw a scaled diagram, and create a stem-and-leaf plot to organize and analyze data, they are using various forms of representation to demonstrate their mathematical thinking. It is important that we give students many opportunities to represent their thinking and guide them to become proficient in representation. As they become more comfortable creating representations of their ideas, their mathematical thinking will greatly expand, as well as their ability to communicate about that thinking.

Representation is both a process and a product by which students are able to explore and sort out mathematical concepts as well as communicate mathematically with their peers. Because representation is both a process and a product, students need many and varied opportunities to explore and sort mathematical concepts and to communicate these concepts to their peers. They need opportunities that will ultimately guide them toward more conventional forms of representation, facilitating their mathematical thinking and deepening their understanding. By enabling students to use a wide variety of representations, we are helping them to assemble a repertoire of tools from which to draw when exploring mathematical concepts.

What Is the Representation Standard?

Principles and Standards for School Mathematics (NCTM 2000) has outlined standards for both math content and math processes. The content standards help us identify key math content that is critical to students' understanding of mathematics, while the process standards help us identify those processes through which students learn and apply math content. Representation is a critical math process that supports students in their learning of math and their ability to express that learning.

In NCTM's original standards document, *Curriculum and Evaluation Standards for School Mathematics* (1989), representation was included as a part of the communication standard, one of the four process standards in the original document. In the 2000 document, five process standards are outlined, with communication and representation individually addressed. NCTM now treats representation as its own process standard in order to address the broad scope of representation and its importance in learning mathematics. It has been recognized that the ability to represent ideas is fundamental to the study of mathematics.

In *Principles and Standards for School Mathematics*, NCTM recommends that instructional programs from prekindergarten through grade 12 should enable all students to—

- create and use representations to organize, record, and communicate mathematical ideas;

- select, apply, and translate among mathematical representations to solve problems; and

- use representations to model and interpret physical, social, and mathematical phenomena.

The abilities to create representations to illustrate ideas, communicate thinking through representations, determine which representation would best fit a concept or idea, and use representation to model math situations are all critical components of this standard.

How Can Representation Support Student Learning?

Representation is both about helping students find their own ways to represent math ideas and about helping them understand conventional representations of math ideas (e.g., fractions, decimals, ratios, expanded notation, charts, graphs, diagrams). Students should be encouraged to represent their ideas in ways that make sense to them. For example, Mrs. Fernandez asked her third-grade students to draw a picture that showed what $3 \times 5 = 15$ meant to them. Julius, a student in that class, drew the representations shown in Figure I–1.

Are these three different representations really examples of the same problem? Do you in fact have five groups of three, or does the problem mean that you have three groups of five? More importantly, does it really matter which representation is used for the multiplication problem? Are the digits in this problem what is most important, or is the students' understanding of the meaning of multiplication more important? In this case, Julius seemed to have a clear understanding of what three times five means and he demonstrated that understanding in a variety of methods. Not only does his

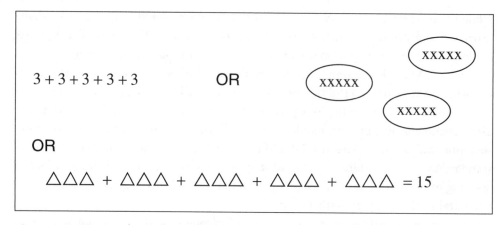

Figure I–1 *Notice that Julius represented the problem 3 × 5 = 15 in three very different ways. Are they all right?*

representation show the value of three times five, but he clearly illustrated that he understood the commutative nature of multiplication. While Julius chose to use numbers and symbols in his answer, others used various pictorial representations to illustrate their thinking. Although many representations are conventional, not all students will show their thinking in conventional ways. It is important that we allow them to work through their thinking in ways that make sense to them and then guide them toward more conventional representations to assist them in better understanding mathematics, as well as to enable others to understand their thought processes.

In this book you will see several examples of ways in which you can provide students with opportunities to represent their thinking and of how to enable them to use those representations in meaningful ways. The process of representation, which is the act of putting one's ideas into words, pictures, numbers, or symbols, is as important as the product: the actual representation of those ideas. We must provide students with many opportunities and ongoing support as they attempt to represent their own ideas and as they explore standard ways to represent math ideas.

In addition to providing students with many opportunities to represent their thinking, we must expose them to a variety of representations. When teaching the concept of division as fair share, Mrs. Davis chose to provide her students with concrete objects such as base ten blocks and counters that they could manipulate to illustrate equal groups. It is important, too, to include in our instruction other ways of representing division, such as through pictures, numbers, and words. In addition, as students' mathematical thinking matures, they learn to choose more appropriate ways of representing their ideas and information. For example, a fifth-grade student, when faced with a set of data, might need to decide which graphical representation would be most appropriate for organizing and then analyzing the data, whether it be a bar graph, a stem-and-leaf plot, a line graph, or a box and whiskers. A third-grade student being asked to demonstrate understanding of the difference between perimeter and area may choose to use the same shape in his representation but identify the different concepts through the appropriate algorithms. By encouraging children to use multiple representations, we help them build a repertoire from which to choose strategies for solving mathematical problems.

Finally, students should use representations to model real-world phenomena. A fourth-grade student might record the daily temperature in her town each day for a month and then represent the data on a line graph in order to effectively analyze it. A third-grade student interested in learning which lunch choice is most popular in the school cafeteria might collect data, select an appropriate graphic representation, and then use that representation to present his findings to his peers, teachers, and principal. Another student might be interested in the relationship between TV watching and school grades, collect data, and represent the correlation graphically, looking for the most appropriate means to demonstrate the findings. Providing students with opportunities to model different phenomena in the world around them leads to a better understanding of that world and to the mathematical relationships within it.

Does Your Classroom Look Like a Math Classroom?

Does your classroom speak math and would someone be able to recognize it as a classroom that places an emphasis on math talk? Many of us have worked hard to have colorful wall displays and bulletin boards made from commercially produced cutouts, but what may be missing is a classroom that clearly said, "This is a math classroom and math is spoken here." Having a room that clearly demonstrates the importance of sharing students' mathematical ideas and work goes a long way in creating a culture that encourages student discourse in the area of mathematics. As teachers we want to make certain that students realize that their math writing and drawings are the most important part of what went goes on in that class on a daily basis.

As teachers we can go from merely asking students to define math concepts using the glossary in the back of their text to having them write the definitions in their own words, representing each concept using an illustration of their choice and finally adding a real-life application that is appropriate for the concept. Moving the class from copying dictionary definitions to representing concepts in multiple forms is not an easy process. Modeling the process in the beginning is essential, and as students began to feel more comfortable with this new way of representing the math, they will look forward to creating their own representations, which for them brings real meaning to the mathematics. Each week students can generate a list of about three to five terms that have been discussed during the week or terms that may have come up during the math lessons. Students can then be allowed to discuss these words in small groups and plan how they think the concepts could best be represented. By working cooperatively on their representations, students will begin to engage more and more in math conversations that will help other students clarify concepts that may still be somewhat fuzzy.

At the same time, students may begin to look for more and more ways to demonstrate the real-life applications of the math for their own representations. This will lead them to search newspapers, magazines, and, yes, even their textbooks for examples they could use to illustrate the math concepts. A wonderful added benefit to this process might become evident at parent conferences. Parents may begin sharing with you ways in which their child is sharing the vocabulary at home. Imagine parents being asked by their child to look at work for examples of math concepts or examples in a newspaper or on the internet. This home-school connection can be an unexpected bonus of the process and a very welcome communication tool that helps parents keep up-to-date on just what topics were being covered during the week. You may also find that by challenging the students to find the real-life applications you now have instant wall displays that become sources of conversation around the mathematics. There will be no doubt about what is valued in your classroom.

Creating a Classroom Environment That Encourages Multiple Student Representations

Teachers can facilitate the process of student representations by creating a classroom that encourages students to represent their math thinking in a variety of ways. One way to encourage a climate of student representation is to provide students with the tools they need to create those representations. Baskets of markers, crayons, and colored pencils to which students have easy access will go a long way in getting students motivated to express their ideas. Because most students in the beginning see representations as drawings, they may be more inclined to create those drawings if they have drawing tools. While it would be great if every classroom had unlimited supplies of easel pads so that students could share their representations for the whole class to see, we all know that isn't the case. One possible solution would be to have bulletin boards covered with brown wrapping paper or any other solid-colored paper and allow students to draw their representations directly on the board.

It is also important that students have an opportunity to share with those around them their interpretations of the mathematics and discuss how their representations help them to understand and illustrate the concepts. A room that encourages communication is one in which students have the ability to work in a cooperative nature, either in small groups or in pairs. When students have the ability not only to discuss the mathematics with their peers but to listen to them explain their thinking, they are more likely to bring their own meaning to the concepts at hand.

C L A S S R O O M - T E S T E D   T I P

As students are working on representing their math ideas, consider putting four desks together and then placing a precut piece of bathroom tile board (from your local building supply store) on top of the four desks, creating an instant work space. The tile board (made of melamine) should have the same dimensions as the four desks combined. Any manipulatives students may be using will not fall through the cracks, and more importantly, with a dry-erase marker, students can create their representations right on the table before they put their finished copy on paper. You can do this for pairs of student desks as well. Students working on the tile board can all do the problem in their own way and then share out at their table. This also makes a great "gallery walk": students can get up and walk around the room, looking at all of the other solutions and representations of the problem.

A note of warning: consider having the edges of the tile board smoothed (using a router or sandpaper) prior to use in order to eliminate sharp edges and corners, and if the boards are too heavy, you might need to help students with picking them up as they put them on top of their desks.

How Can the Use of Representations Help All Populations?

Classrooms today are becoming increasingly diverse. With added ELL (English language learner) populations as well as the increasingly inclusive nature of all classrooms, it is more important than ever to meet the needs of a wide range of student abilities. At the same time as teachers are becoming more cognizant of the research associated with learning styles, finding ways to reach those learners is crucial. Teachers who encourage students to represent their mathematical thinking in a variety of ways can help meet the needs of those students who may find difficulty in explaining or writing down their thinking in words. Students needing alternate ways of expressing their thinking oftentimes find that pictorial representations open a much-needed path for communication. For example, an ELL student will find it much easier to solve a problem that is presented to him pictorially rather than just written out. Likewise, a teacher is much more likely to see a student's thinking when the steps in her solution are either drawn out or written in numeric fashion. The same holds true for special education students working in an inclusive classroom. When the entire class is involved in looking at the math through mathematical models and being encouraged to represent their answers in like fashion, all students feel included and do not feel that they are being singled out for alternate instruction. The key is to have all students feeling comfortable with this process and feeling equal in their ability to understand and communicate the mathematics. Students need to understand that when they are asked to "explain their answer" and "show their work," there are a number of ways in which they can do so.

C L A S S R O O M - T E S T E D   T I P

As students become more comfortable in sharing their ideas with others, it is important to make sure all students have an opportunity to participate in an equal fashion. For that reason, equity sticks are a useful tool in any classroom. From a craft department, purchase craft sticks at the beginning of the year and write each student's name on one of the sticks. As you work through a lesson and question the students, reach into the container, pull out an equity stick, and call on the student whose name is written on the stick.

A word of caution in using the sticks: If you have a reluctant learner or a shy student who may not want to answer out loud for fear of being wrong, work out a signal with him or her ahead of time so they can communicate with you whether or not they want to answer prior to calling their name. If you see this signal and know the student feels comfortable enough to answer out loud, then no matter whose name is on the stick that is pulled out of the cup, you can call on your reluctant learner. As an added bonus, equity sticks are a great way to help teachers learn student names at the beginning of the year.

Considerations in Lesson Planning

Ongoing attention to lesson design also helps to create an environment in which students feel comfortable representing their math ideas with pictures, tables, numbers, or manipulatives. Planning lessons that routinely include higher-order questioning, cooperative group work, and class discussions set the stage for productive representation. The use of manipulatives, the posing of problems, and the reading of math-related literature each provide a stimulus for representing math ideas. A balance of whole-group activities, small teacher-led groups, cooperative groups, partner work, and independent tasks provides for varied opportunities for students to develop their representation skills.

In planning lessons, it is important to allow enough time for students to explore math ideas and ways to represent those ideas. Asking follow-up questions that uncover students' reasoning or procedures is vital. Posing fewer tasks but allocating time to discuss ideas and solutions builds students' reasoning and problem-solving skills. Structuring assignments with fewer rote tasks and more reasoning helps balance students' skill development. To ensure that students are not hurried, make sure to allow time for them to share ideas with others prior to beginning an independent task or, in some instances spend a few minutes modeling representations prior to assigning an independent task.

Creating an environment that promotes communication is about modifying our expectations from quiet students to verbal students and from correct answers to reflective thinking. It is about developing a community of learners who respect each other's ideas, whether right or wrong, and who work to support each other in building math understanding.

How This Book Will Help You

This book is designed to help you better understand the representation process standard and its significance. While the book is specifically designed for teachers in grades 3 through 5 and correlates with math content generally taught at those levels, teachers at other grade levels may find strategies and activity ideas that can be used with their students as well. In each section the standards are explained and illustrated through a variety of student work samples, and practical ideas are shared for helping students develop their skills in representing mathematical information, as well as tools to assist you in assessing students' representations.

In Chapter 1, "How Representations Support Learning," a variety of strategies are presented that illustrate the importance of providing students with opportunities to create representations that make the math meaningful to them. The chapter also offers up some suggested interpretations teachers might make about the levels of student understanding just from looking at the student representations. In addition, you will find some practical applications for getting at student representations for various strands of mathematics such as the use of Venn diagrams in a variety of problem-solving situations and at various levels of cognitive demand. Logic problems and their significance in helping students organize solutions in a systematic way are discussed.

Chapter 2, "Using Manipulatives to Model and Illustrate Key Math Concepts," takes a closer look at how the use of manipulatives can guide students as they develop their own representations for the math at hand. Manipulatives are a staple in all math classes. Whether these tools are store-bought or teacher created, the research is clear on their importance. Whether it is in geometry or number computation, manipulatives can provide students with a model that will help them internalize a concept and then enable them to create their own model and interpretation of the math concept. This chapter also provides classroom examples of how the connection between the concrete manipulative and the student representation can be used to build student understanding.

Chapter 3, "Using Pictures and Diagrams to Represent Mathematical Thinking," will take you through two of the most difficult concepts for students at these grade levels and offer some suggestions on how to use proven instructional strategies to help students clarify concepts and processes related to fractions and division. Using a key reading strategy such as *before, during, and after*, teachers may find a way to provide their students with an avenue for representing the mathematics that will help them build on prior knowledge and connect that knowledge to new processes.

In the next chapter, "Using Numbers and Symbols to Represent Mathematical Ideas," the value of student-invented algorithms is explored as well as ways to use them to support student learning. Moving students from the pictorial to the numeric representation of the mathematics is ultimately the goal in any math classroom, but helping students make the connections and bring meaning to the math is a crucial process and one that cannot be rushed.

Developing student understanding of how to graph specific types of data is discussed in Chapter 5, "Using Tables and Graphs to Record, Organize, and Communicate Ideas." Whether graphing information on a line graph or a stem-and-leaf plot, students need to understand and see the various data representations used so that they have the skill to choose the appropriate representations for any type of data.

Chapter 6, "Assessing Students' Representations," looks at how teachers can make decisions about assessments as they apply to the representation standard. Finally, in Chapter 7, "Representation Across the Content Standards," we share lesson ideas to illustrate the representation process standard as it connects to the teaching of numbers and operations, algebra, geometry, measurement, and data and probability. Engaging students in representing their mathematical thinking in all content standards will ensure their success in applying the process in other areas.

At the end of each chapter we include questions that can be used for individual reflection or to generate faculty study group discussions. The accompanying CD provides a variety of practical resources you can use to help your students more effectively represent their math ideas, including lesson ideas that can easily be adapted to meet your individual needs. This book will expand your understanding of the representation standard and will provide you with the practical resources that you'll need to implement the ideas with your students. You will also be able to take the activities on the CD and personalize them for use in your classroom. All along the way, the "Classroom-Tested Tip" boxes will provide examples of time-saving, student-motivating, and curriculum-enhancing ideas that come from the classrooms of experienced math teachers. They are designed to make classroom management and instruction a little easier and more meaningful, and to send the message that, yes, math can be fun!

Each chapter builds on the previous chapter but can also stand alone if you are looking for one or two ideas to help math instruction in your classroom. As you read through, keep this in mind: This book is written by math teachers for math teachers, with the hope that as you read through the book, at some point in time you'll have that *aha* moment and you will say to yourself, "That just might work!"

Questions for Discussion

1. What does it mean to say that representation can be both a process and a product?

2. How can representing math ideas help students strengthen their understanding of math?

3. How can attention to students' representations help teachers better assess students' understanding?

4. What are some of the physical characteristics of a math classroom where students are encouraged to freely represent math ideas?

5. How can students be encouraged to communicate mathematically through representations?

6. How can the classroom environment encourage a climate of student representation?

CHAPTER 1

How Representations Support Learning

The Value of Understanding How to Represent Math Ideas

Stop for a minute, close your eyes, and picture in your mind that one math problem that frustrated you as a student. It made your palms sweat and even today just the thought of having to tackle it can cause waves of anxiety. For most of us it probably has something to do with trains A and B leaving two stations. Today more than ever, our students are confronted with complex problem-solving situations that for them can create that same level of consternation. Our goal as teachers is to guide them, coach them, and encourage them as they develop their problem-solving skills and then communicate their solutions to others.

One way to achieve this goal is to show them the power of drawing pictures and using numbers, words, graphic organizers, and manipulatives alone or in combinations to bring real meaning to the problems. In short, the ability to create multiple representations in solving any type of math problem cannot be underestimated. When students have the confidence to represent problems in a variety of ways, they truly bring a sense of understanding and ownership to the mathematics around them.

Organizing Information

Learning to record or represent thinking in an organized way, both in solving a problem and in sharing a solution, is an acquired skill for many students (NCTM 2000).

How many times have we stood helplessly by and watched a student or group of students try to work through a seemingly easy problem that they have not been able to solve? They have either missed the solution because of unorganized trials and errors or failed to see how close they were to the actual solution because of haphazard notations. Perhaps the answer was right in front of their eyes, but because of the disorganized nature of their work, it went unnoticed. This is especially true when the answer is more easily found by discovering a function or pattern in the data that ultimately leads to a solution. Problems with multiple constraints can give students a difficult time if they are not careful to consider the whole problem instead of trying to solve it one part at a time.

Consider the following problem:

Driving by a farm, I saw chickens and cows. Through the fence I counted a total of 40 legs and 15 heads. How many chickens and cows did I see?

This is one of those relatively easy problems for students at this level to solve, but when working on it, they may find it difficult to see a pattern in their trials and errors if they don't make an effort to organize their work in some type of table or matrix. Students would certainly more easily recognize the solution if they used an organizational structure that allowed them to keep track of all of their trials.

Students using a table such as the one in Figure 1–1 should be able to see after a couple of guesses which direction to go with their next guess. Keeping track of and organizing the trials would ultimately lead them to see that each time you decrease the number of cows and increase the number of chickens by the same number, the number of legs decreases proportionally. They may not be able to express it in those terms, but that isn't important at this stage of the game. The goal would be to find the solution with fewer guesses but also bring a sense of importance to putting their guesses down in an organizational pattern. True, the first guess is just that—a guess—but understanding how that first guess relates to the problem as a whole and the relationship between the first and second guess to the ultimate solution is paramount. The solution can be found more quickly (always a selling point with students) when they look at the work in a sequential manner instead of putting guesses all over the paper. When the work is organized, the relationship of the parts of the problem is much more evident, bringing real meaning to the mathematics.

There is no doubt that this type of table is useful in recording trials and errors, but it also records for the teacher the thinking that occurred as the students were engaged in solving the problem. Whether they were using manipulatives, drawing pictures, or using another problem-solving tool, the thinking is revealed in the record keeping of the trials. Going back and asking, "Do you remember what you were thinking with this guess?" or "Why did you decide to try this number next?" would be impossible to if the student didn't keep any record of the trials and errors.

Animals	☒ Trial 1	☒ Trial 2	☑ Trial 3
Cows	10 heads × 4 legs	8 heads × 4 legs	5 heads × 4 legs
Chickens	5 heads × 2 legs	7 heads × 2 legs	10 heads × 2 legs
Total Legs	50 legs	46 legs	40 legs
Total Heads	15 heads	15 heads	15 heads

Figure 1–1 *An organized table can help students solve problems.*

Some students may choose to solve this problem by representing the chickens and the cows pictorially instead of using a matrix of trials. The challenge here is to get at students' thinking as they work through the problem. Unless a student makes a conscious effort to communicate their trials, there is no way to see the progression of thought. The other downfall of representing the problem pictorially is the time that it would take to arrive at the solution. Encourage students to look at the possibility of creating iconic representations to speed up the process.

When Kurt approached this problem, he began by drawing the fifteen heads because he said he knew he had fifteen animals and they all had one head. He then began by giving each animal two legs because, as he said, "I know they all have at least two legs and so then I used thirty legs." Once he gave each animal two legs, he then began to distribute the remaining ten legs, two at a time, until he had used all of the remaining legs. This gave him the correct solution of five cows and ten chickens, and he then embellished his representations a little to make them look like cows and chickens. This is a great solution but difficult to evaluate without talking to the student. So the challenge here is to get the student to represent the solution but also represent the steps in the solution so you can get a good picture (no pun intended!).

Taylor had another approach to the problem. He started by seeing how many cows he could get with forty legs and found the answer: ten. He then determined that every cow was equivalent to two chickens in terms of number of legs, and so as he took away one cow, he added two chickens and repeated the process until he had fifteen heads. (See Figure 1–2.)

The following examples can all be used to help students see a progression of trials and errors as they work through the problems.

1. A furniture maker was putting stools and chairs together. The stools were the three-legged kind and the chairs had four legs. If the seats were the same for the stools and chairs, how many of each could he make if he had 21 seats and 72 legs?

2. A bicycle maker was putting together bikes and tricycles. Assuming that the handlebars and wheels could be used on either one, how many of each could he make with 15 sets of handlebars and 39 wheels?

3. Sue looked out her schoolroom window and saw a group of pigeons and squirrels. She counted all the legs of the pigeons and squirrels and found that the total number of legs add up to 66. How many of each kind of animal (pigeons and squirrels) passed by her window if the total number of animals was 24?

There are endless possibilities in working with problems of this nature. Students should find the problems easy to represent but also easy to create. Having students solve problems created by classmates adds an element of fun to the process. It also forces the creator to take care in making sure all of the numbers add up.

Using logic problems in a math classroom allows students an opportunity to practice their step-by-step problem-solving skills. Students engaged in solving logic problems such as those dealing with deductive reasoning skills would find it almost

Name: _____

Farm Dilemma

One afternoon I visited my grandparent's farm. As we drove up to
the farm I could see chickens and cows through the fenced in
pasture. Through the fence, I counted a total of 40 legs and 15
heads. How many chickens and cows did I see?

5 cows   10 chickens

Show your work.

1 cow = 2 chickens   10 cows = 40 legs = 10 heads
9 + 2 = 11
8 + 4 = 12
                                    5
    .   .   .   +10
                                  15 heads

5 cows 10 chickens   5 × 4 = 20 legs
                       10 + 10 = 20 legs

Explain how you solved the problem.

First I found how many cows fit into
40. I know 1 cow = 2 chicks so every time
I took away a cow I te two chicks
till I got 15 heads.

Challenge: If 4 more cows and 12 more chickens were put in the
pasture what would the total number of heads and legs be now?

4 + 12 = 18 + 15 = 33 heads

1 cow = 4 legs   4 12   1 chick = 2 legs
                 ×4 ×2
                 16 + 24 = 40 + 40 = 80 legs

Figure 1–2 *Taylor's work*

impossible to reach an accurate conclusion in a timely fashion without the use of a table
or matrix. It is essential they have the ability to record the information given so that
they can start eliminating the impossible situations first. Consider the following problem:

> Five skiers were finishing a race. From the following information, can you tell
> how Al, Barbara, and Dion placed in the race?
> Carol placed third and Evan placed second.
> Al was not last. Al came in after Evan. Dion was not first.

In this example, students would start with what is given. Therefore, if Al was not
last, students could eliminate that choice and also eliminate the first-place choice for
Al since the problem states he came in after Evan. Because the problem tells us that
Carol placed third and Evan placed second, Al must have come in fourth. The last clue

	First	Second	Third	Fourth	Fifth
Al	no	no	no	yes	no
Barbara	yes	no	no	no	no
Carol	no	no	yes	no	no
Dion	no	no	no	no	yes
Evan	no	yes	no	no	no

Figure 1–3 *Matrix for race problem*

means that Barbara must have come in first since she and Dion are the only possible choices left and the problem tells us that Dion wasn't first. If Barbara came in first, Dion had to have finished the race last. Figure 1–3 shows the completed solution. Logic problems such as these hold so much value in training students to start with what is given and then work through the problem step-by-step before reaching a conclusion. The catch here is getting students to avoid premature conclusions. Some students jump to conclusions before they have sufficient information, and once they make an incorrect assumption, it is almost impossible to correctly finish the problem. Solving deductive reasoning problems such as these is a much-needed precursor skill for algebra. The value of organizing information during any mathematical situation cannot be underestimated. It is through this process that students bring meaning to the situation and communicate their understanding of the problem at hand. The hard part for students here is communicating solutions in order. Once the problem is done, do they have any idea what they did first, second, third, or last? Sometimes sticky notes or highlighter markers can be used to keep track of that information, or students can try to number their steps as they work through the problem.

In Mrs. Robbins' fifth-grade class, deductive reasoning puzzles are done on a regular basis, with students creating the matrices from the problems given. As a part of their regular problem-solving activities, students work either independently or in small groups to create the matrix and work through the problem. Here's an example of the problems they work with:

> **Five people play in a band. The instruments include a clarinet, drums, a flute, a saxophone, and a trumpet. The names of the band members are John, Paul, George, Ringo, and Mick. Use the clues to determine who plays what instrument.**
>
> n **John plays the saxophone.**
>
> n **George does not play an instrument that uses wind.**
>
> n **Ringo does not play the flute or the clarinet.**
>
> n **Paul's instrument is held sideways when it is played.**

Students working in small groups set the problem up by first counting the number of categories needed to create the matrix. Joe commented that since there were five people and five instruments, the matrix needed to be six by six. Once students had the grid drawn, they set to work labeling each of the squares. Carla wondered if it mattered whether the names went across the top or down the side. Since Mrs. Robbins wanted students to try to answer their own questions, the group decided that as long as one side had the names and the other side had the instruments, it shouldn't matter which side they used for which category. David compared the matrix to a multiplication chart and said that since order didn't matter in a multiplication table, it shouldn't matter here.

The group began putting checks and *X*'s in the squares as they read the clues. The first check was in the box that intersected John and saxophone, and that meant that an *X* needed to go in all other boxes in that column and row. Since the problem said George doesn't play an instrument that uses wind, the students put a check in the box for drum. The saxophone had already been ruled out for George since it was already determined that John played that instrument. The kids put *X*'s in the flute and clarinet boxes for Ringo and a final check in the box for Paul and flute, since that is the only instrument that is held sideways when it is played. The only other boxes remaining were for Mick and the clarinet and Ringo and the trumpet. The group finished their matrix and shared their response with the rest of the class.

Venn Diagrams

The Venn diagram is another tool that enables students to organize information such as the attributes of shapes, aspects of data, common factors and multiples, or the similarities and differences of numbers and shapes. It is also a valuable tool that can be used in problem-solving situations. Students just beginning work with Venn diagrams can start with a single circle and a question or survey with only two choices: either it is or it isn't. For example, earlier grades can start with topics such as shoes that tie, shoes that don't tie; shirts with buttons, shirts with no buttons; or students who buy lunch and students who pack their lunch. With a single circle, the inside could be one of the two characteristics and the outside would be the other. Venn diagrams can be made more complex with the addition of more circles, allowing for additional sets or elements to be compared. In multicircle Venn diagrams, each region represents one attribute or characteristic, and the overlapping region of two or more circles represents those attributes the elements have in common. Outside the circles is yet another area that can be used to represent those numbers, shapes, or pieces of data that do not belong to any group. In addition to determining common characteristics, Venn diagrams can be used to help students with some numeric processes. Students asked to find common multiples of two numbers could organize their information using a Venn diagram so that the common multiples could be easily recognized, or the diagrams could provide an alternate method of simplifying fractions. Consider the following situation: Find the multiples and common multiples of six and eight. Using a Venn diagram such as the one in Figure 1–4, students would first identify the multiples of six and place them in circle A. The multiples of eight would be placed in circle B. Any multiples found to be in both circles would then be placed in the region where the two circles overlapped.

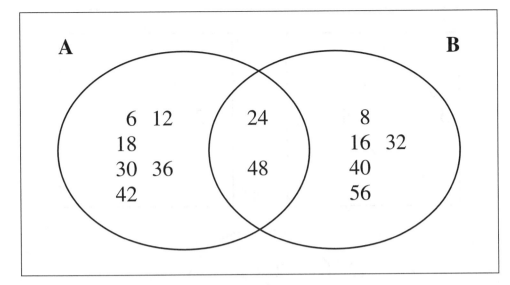

Figure 1–4 *Venn diagram showing the multiples of six and eight*

Students using this Venn diagram would have no trouble picking out the common multiples, twenty-four and forty-eight, as well as the least common multiple (LCM), twenty-four. This organizational tool works in a number of situations, such as solving computational problems involving fractions needing common denominators, but it is made more powerful when students have an opportunity to choose the attributes or characteristics each circle will represent.

The Venn can also be rotated around so that it looks like one circle in on top of the other (see Figure 1–5). In this example, students can use the Venn to help determine whether a fraction has been stated in simplest form. For example, if the students were looking at the fraction twelve-fifteenths, they would start by doing the prime factorization for both numbers. Once they had the factors of both, they would put them in the diagram, with the common factors in the middle.

Since both numbers have a prime factor of three, that number would go in the intersection of the two circles, as in Figure 1–5, with the remaining numbers going in the individual sections of each circle. If a section had more than one prime factor, you would multiply them to find the product of those factors.

The end result would be a fraction in its simplest form, four-fifths, since the three is the common factor. Using this representation, students can visualize the process of what it means to factor numbers and how the common factors can be removed from the original numbers.

Geometry is another area where students can make use of the Venn diagram. Working with attribute blocks, pattern blocks, or geometric shapes, students could be instructed to place the pieces in one of the regions of the Venn diagram using criteria that they establish. Not only do they have to choose the attributes by which to sort the shapes, but they have to be able to communicate those decisions to someone looking at their organizer.

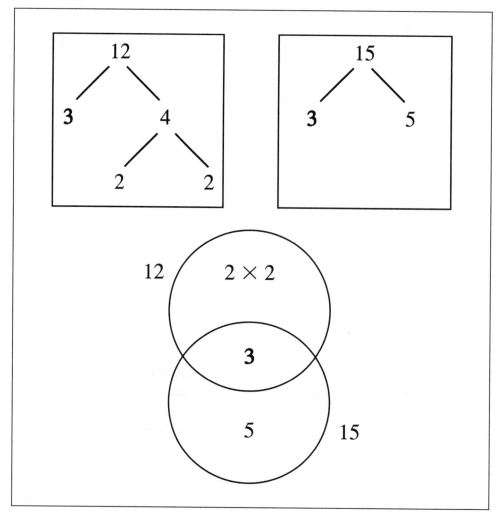

Figure 1–5 *Finding simplest form of a fraction*

Students in Mrs. Savoy's third-grade math class were asked to place shapes in one of the regions of the diagram and then explain their decision. Figure 1–6 shows how one student, Rachel, arranged her shapes.

It is important to remember to give students the opportunity to make these decisions and allow time for the communication instead of always giving them the characteristics of each circle. Even though a student's thinking might not always be what we were expecting, there is so much value in allowing students time to work through all of these steps and to process their own decisions. In this case, Rachel wrote that she put the pieces with at least one straight side in one circle and shapes that had rounded sides in the other. She continued by saying that since one shape had both a straight side and a rounded edge, it went in the space between the two circles. She also concluded that the pieces with "dented" edges should go on the outside. It is important for students to identify the attributes of these geometric shapes that create the similarities and differences and determine if there are other ways to group the shapes. One important question to ask would be, "What criteria did you use in placing the shapes outside the Venn?" Students might respond with comments similar to

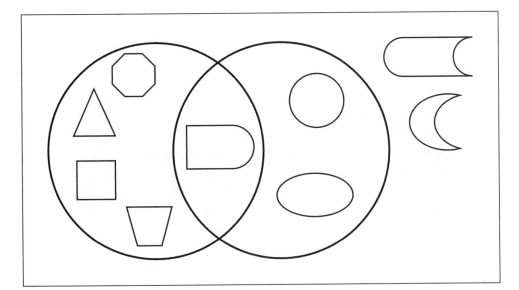

Figure 1–6 *Rachel's Venn diagram*

Rachel's and describe the shapes as dented. While the concepts of concave and convex may not have been the focus of this particular lesson, students need to feel confident that when they make these decisions and communicate them appropriately, they will be accepted. The vocabulary now becomes more meaningful for the students since they have had time to internalize the concept. It is important for teachers to encourage and accept multiple answers in situations such as this so that students feel more comfortable thinking outside the box. It also provides additional opportunities for those teachable moments we all love.

Once students have had ample opportunities to work with the Venn diagram in multiple problem-solving situations, you can increase the level of difficulty by adding a third circle to the diagram, similar to the one in Figure 1–7. Problems using a third circle can be challenging to say the least, and it is important for the teacher to model their use at first before turning students loose on their own. There are some great problems using three circles available on the CD.

Students in Miss Elliott's fifth-grade class tackled the following problem during a whole-class activity: Fifth-grade students completed a survey of the after-school sports they played. According to the survey, a total of fifty-four students played basketball, thirty-two students played football, and seventy-six students played soccer. The teacher posed this problem:

If fourteen of those students played just basketball and soccer, six played just basketball and football, twenty played just football and soccer, and five students played all three sports, how many students played just one sport?

Naturally, the students immediately started adding and subtracting numbers, forgetting for a moment the tool that they were working with in this case was the triple Venn diagram. Their teacher quickly reminded them that since they had the diagram, they needed to first look at the information that was given and fill in the sections that they could. The students started by labeling the three circles "football," "basketball," and "soccer" and then putting the totals in each of the portions of the intersecting circles. Then they worked their way to the outside circles for the final answers. As they worked their way to the outside sections, they had to remember to continue to include the previous numbers in their totals. For example, since five students played all three sports, then the students had to remember to include those five students in the totals for each of the three sports. They also needed to include the students playing two sports in each of the totals for the individual sports. The final count for individual sports was thirty-seven students played just soccer, twenty-nine students played just basketball, and only one student played just football. Miss Elliott asked them to go back to the original question and check their answers to make sure they had not counted a student twice. Bruce's group showed their check as follows:

> *Statement 1: Fifty-four students played basketball. Our numbers: 29 + 14 + 5 + 6 = 54* √
>
> *Statement 2: Thirty-two students played football. Our numbers: 20 + 5 + 6 + 1 = 32* √
>
> *Statement 3: Seventy-six students played soccer. Our numbers: 14 + 5 + 20 + 37 = 76* √

They then checked their Venn diagram against the remaining numbers, and since no numbers needed to be added, they concluded that they had checked everything needed.

An added challenge to this type of problem would be to have students start with the numbers for each sport and pairs of sports and then determine the total number of students in the survey.

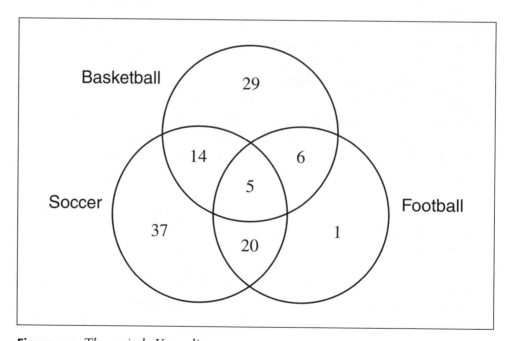

Figure 1–7 *Three-circle Venn diagram*

If you are looking for a way to add a little fun to the use of the Venn diagram and meet the needs of some of your more kinesthetic learners, hula hoops make great Venn diagram circles. They can be placed on the floor or attached to the chalkboard. Students can represent their answers by putting the shapes, numbers, cards, manipulatives, or themselves inside the circles. If your chalkboard is also magnetic, attach small magnets to the back of the cards and students can take turns placing answers in the appropriate sections. Purchasing a roll of magnetic tape and cutting it into pieces is an economical way to accomplish this task. This is a great way to get students up and moving!

Recording Ideas or Observations

Students actively engaged in creating their own notes and observations bring a keen sense of understanding to the mathematics, as opposed to those students copying teacher-created notes. In order for students to construct their own knowledge and understandings about the mathematics, they need to be active participants. Passive learners aren't working to create new ideas and connections, and while it is sometimes easier to just give students the information as they work through an investigation, the only person constructing meaning from the material in that case is the teacher. We can't tell students how to think; we can't be the authors of their ideas and observations. What we can do is create a community of mathematicians that sees value in being able to connect information, gleaned from investigations or experiments, to the abstract mathematical concepts that will make them successful in connecting to skills and concepts with a higher level of cognitive demand. To this end, we need to encourage students to observe, process the information, and note what is important to remember. Easier said than done! How do you create this community of self-assured mathematicians eager to observe and record with the eye of an investigative reporter?

One way is to provide an early note-taking structure to classroom lessons or investigations and encourage students to develop a system of representations that makes sense to them. Students can be supported in the beginning with templates that allow them ways to zero in on what's important. A chart, a diagram, or simply a set of guiding questions to use as they work through the process goes a long way toward helping them develop good mathematical communication.

As students are working on new material, have them set their paper up in two columns. One column could be for the examples and the second column could be designated for the work section, or one column could be set up for note taking and the second column for examples and pictorial representations of the vocabulary. There are several models that utilize this strategy and there are just as many names for those strategies. In one model, students divide their paper into four sections and on one section they write a word, in a second section they create an example of the vocabulary word, in the third section they draw a picture of the term, and in the fourth section students describe a real-world application for the term. Giving students the

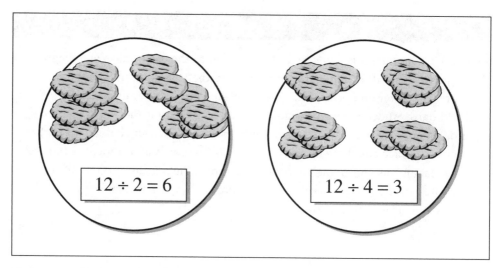

Figure 1–8 *Representing the story in* The Doorbell Rang

opportunity to relate the mathematics to a real-world application is important for long-term retention. Without the connection, the math is sometimes forgotten.

Another way to bring structure to students' work and help them organize their work is to provide note-taking structure that relates to the concept or, in this case, a math-related literature piece. Students ready to make the leap from manipulative use to mathematical notation in division might benefit from hearing the now familiar story *The Doorbell Rang*, by Pat Hutchins (1986). As the students listened to the story being read, they could use a template that resembled a cookie tray to help them record their ideas and notations. Each student in the cooperative group could have a different tray on which the individual or group would record the mathematics found in the story and connect the numbers with a picture or manipulative (see Figure 1–8). This record, which could help students keep track of the mathematics found in this story, would be a powerful tool in helping them make the connections between the concrete manipulative or picture and the abstract algorithm.

Here the recording of the mathematical sentences could begin to take students to another level as they brought meaning and understanding to division. As they moved to this new level, they may even begin to feel confident enough to record the steps numerically or switch to an iconic representation for the manipulative instead of feeling the need to always draw realistic pictures. Using iconic representations such as circles or *X*'s would certainly speed up the process.

CLASSROOM-TESTED TIP

Use plastic trays or plates made from melamine for students to record their answers. Using a dry-erase marker, students can write directly onto the surface of the plate. This brings an unexpected element of fun to the activity. The writing wipes right off, and inexpensive sets of white socks work great as erasers. The sock is also a handy place to store the marker, and small plates and markers can be stored in zip-top bags for future use. Smooth placemats work also for an activity like this, although you may find you need to use dry-erase spray to eliminate the shadow marks from the surface once you erase. You'll find many uses for these plates, and seasonal plates and placemats can add an extra dimension of fun to the activity.

Perimeter and area are two of those related concepts that students always seem to confuse. One reason may be the way the two concepts are taught. Most curricula present the two concepts in tandem because of their relationship to one another. Do our students have enough experiences with one concept before we introduce the second concept? What if students had multiple opportunities to experience activities with only perimeter before we introduced area? Brain research tells us that students who are actively engaged in constructing meaning are more likely to retain and internalize that information. For this reason, providing students with meaningful tasks that require them to interact with the mathematics in a variety of settings will ensure students can transfer that knowledge to higher-level skills. Another great story for reinforcing the skill of recording ideas as students work through a problem is *Spaghetti and Meatballs for All!* by Marilyn Burns (1997). It is a story about a couple wanting to have a dinner for their friends and family. As the story progresses, the number of available seats (perimeter) changes but the number of tables (area) remains constant. Activities related to this book can engage students in thinking about the way area and perimeter are related to one another and how a change in one may or may not change the other. Using this book with students also provides a real-world application of the concepts. As students listen to the story, they should be provided with manipulatives that simulate the tables and chairs. Favorite manipulatives for this activity are small square crackers to represent the tables and goldfish crackers to represent the chairs. Because the situation changes from one page to the next, it is important for students to record the situations as they change. Using large-grid graph paper, students can draw the table-and-seat arrangements from one page to the next. The discussion that takes place after the story ends is crucial to making sure students conceptualize the differences in the two concepts. Questions might include "What happens to the number of seats when the first set of tables are pushed together?" Students can be prompted to compare the number of tables with the number of seats without making reference to the words *area* and *perimeter*. The hope here is that students will be able to make the important connection between the two concepts using a real-world example.

Communicate, Communicate, Communicate

One of the most frustrating phrases for a math teacher to hear is "I don't know how I did it. I just did it in my head." Trying to pull those thoughts and ideas out of our students' heads and get them down on paper can be a challenging task to say the least. The trick here is to make it meaningful and somewhat fun for the students to communicate their thinking. Engaging students in opportunities to express their ideas and solutions in alternate ways can provide the motivation needed to get the ideas on paper and also play to the strengths of diverse learners.

When students are given a problem to solve or challenge to investigate, we can encourage them to do the representation in a number of different ways. For example, one group of students could be challenged to solve the problem strictly using an appropriate algorithm; another group can show the solution pictorially using an iconic symbol or more realistic picture; another group might be challenged to find a way to chart the solution; and of course other groups could use manipulatives to represent the solution. Student groups can then report to the rest of the group using their given representation style. Those presentations can bring about choruses of "I didn't think of that" and "That way looks way easier than our way. I'm going to try it that way next time."

Students challenged with the following problem involving division and the interpretation of the remainder might choose a number of different representations to communicate their solution.

> On a recent field trip, students brought drinks to have during the break and stored them in coolers to keep them cold. If each of the 23 students in the group brought 1 drink and each cooler held 6 drinks, how many coolers would be needed?

Students using numerical representations could write the traditional algorithm: 23 ÷ 6 = 3 r 5. Interpreting the remainder correctly would mean that the students must be able to identify the need for four coolers instead of saying the answer is three remainder five, as so many times happens when students are given a problem such as this one and they answer using only the numerical solution. Having students write their explanation out once they have solved the problem is essential for getting to the correct solution.

Students using pictorial representations might draw coolers with drinks inside. Drawing a cooler and "filling it up" with six cans before moving on to the next cooler would get them to the correct solution. See Figure 1–9.

Students using this method would then be able to not only interpret the remainder correctly but also tell how many drinks ultimately ended up in the last cooler.

Still others might choose to start with twenty-three symbols for the drinks and circle groups of six. See Figure 1–10.

Whatever method students use to show their solution, the key is getting it out of their heads and on the paper. Initially students will have great difficulty with this skill.

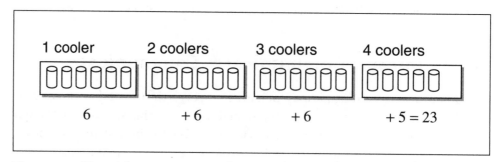

Figure 1–9 *Pictorial representation of twenty-three drinks in four coolers*

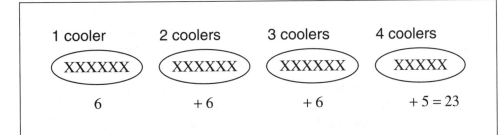

Figure 1–10 *Symbolic representation of drinks and coolers*

With the manipulatives on their desk and the solution in their heads, a teacher will need to coax them to write the solution on the paper. One strategy that works well in cooperative groups is to designate the recorder to write down not only the final answer but also the steps in the process. The more opportunities students have to practice this process and the more opportunities they have to see alternate solution representations, the more likely they are to feel comfortable about their abilities to put their thinking on paper. Students possessing these skills are more apt to tackle problems at a higher level of demand.

Using Representations to Model a Process or Concept

It is important to remember that students must be able to construct meaning and internalize the many mathematical processes and concepts that they are expected to learn. Only through that internalization of the process will it ever go beyond that rote memorization level that we all know results in "Our teacher didn't teach us that last year!" What they really mean is that it was taught, but they just don't remember. We spend a great deal of time chastising the teachers in the previous grade levels for not making sure students knew their multiplication tables, how to divide, or how to add and subtract fractions instead of reflecting on our own practice. Are we guilty of doing the same things? Students provided with opportunities to internalize a process through modeling problem-solving situations instead of just practicing the process over and over again are much more likely to remember and to be able to apply the process when confronted with higher-level problems. "Students need to work with each representation extensively in many contexts as well as move between representations in order to understand how they can use a representation to model mathematical ideas and relationships" (NCTM 2000).

Grades 3 through 5 are critical years for students as they refine and extend their skills with multiplication, division, fractions, and decimals. One of the most widely used manipulative models for place value are base ten blocks. One of the reasons these work so well is that they are already proportional in size and come with ready-made grouped sets of tens, hundreds, and thousands. Students using these models to learn addition, subtraction, and place value can literally see the relationships between the values by comparing the sizes of the pieces. Trading in ten ones for one ten or ten tens for one hundred becomes more meaningful because the of size relationship of the pieces. The physical size of the pieces can serve as a cue to the number relationship between the values. However, that same model becomes more difficult to use in grades 3 through 5 once the numbers students are working with become larger and more complex. There are times when students can be encouraged to make the problem smaller, but that is sometimes not appropriate for the work at hand. It is important to find ways to help students generalize the magnitude of numbers and place values beyond what they can see with the standard manipulative models. For this reason, we need to engage them in activities that showcase the size of large numbers, and at the same time we need to make sure they can relate to the size of those numbers that are less than one.

Developing number sense during the primary grades using the models at hand can help students as they work with larger numbers, but generalizations are not enough. How many classes have started collecting a million bottle caps only to find that the task was too unwieldy or just impossible from a standpoint of finding some place to store the collected caps? Perhaps an easier activity would be to collect ten thousand and then one hundred thousand and then work to help students generalize the number using the grouping model. As students collect the bottle caps, they need to find a system for keeping track of the amounts. Using tally marks allows students to group quantities of the items as they are collected and then translate the symbolic representation to numerical representation. A number of literature books, such as Jerry Pallotta's *Count to a Million* (2003), David Schwartz's *How Much Is a Million?* (1993), and Helen Nolan's *How Much, How Many, How Far, How Heavy, How Long, How Tall Is 1,000?* (2001), focus on larger quantities and help students gain a true sense of the size of those numbers. Using these books in a math classroom helps make that ever important math-literature connection. Additional titles are listed in the "Resources for Teachers" section of this book.

The Role of the Teacher

One of the most important things we need to remember about graphic organizers or any other organizational tool students might use is that they need to see how the tool can be used for multiple purposes. For example, if students see a Venn diagram used only in reading class for comparing and contrasting, they won't be likely to use it in math class. Seeing the similarities and differences in math concepts and processes is a crucial process in helping students remember and internalize them. Students duplicating an organizer in the same manner that they have seen it modeled may be getting meaning from that process. On the other hand, they may just be copying what they have seen the teacher produce. Allow students an opportunity not only to see various organizers in use but also to choose which ones they want to use for a given situation.

Questions for Discussion

1. Venn diagrams and matrices help students organize their thoughts and trials as they work through problem-solving situations. What other graphic organizers lend themselves to this best practice?

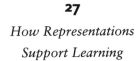

Support Learning

Figure 1-11 *Students in Miss Elliott's class work together to complete their Venn diagram.*

2. What other benefits can be found in making the math-literature connection?

3. What problems encourage students to respond using multiple representations?

4. How can graphic organizers be used to differentiate a problem-solving situation?

2

Using Manipulatives to Model and Illustrate Key Math Concepts

Mathematical representations help provide students with a perspective on phenomena.

—Sara P. Fisher and Christopher Hartmann, "Math Through the Mind's Eye"

Modeling Ideas with Manipulatives

The National Council of Teachers of Mathematics recommends that teachers should employ "representations to model and interpret physical, social, and mathematical phenomena" (NCTM 2000, 70) and that students should use mathematical representations to organize their thinking and reflect on numerical or geometric information. In the previous chapter, we discussed how different representations support mathematical learning. As students become more comfortable creating models of their thinking, they build a repertoire of strategies from which to pull when faced with a novel task. "The very act of generating a concrete representation establishes an image of the knowledge in students' minds," writes Marzano et al. (2001, 78). In this chapter, we look at the power of using manipulatives to help students develop their own understanding of mathematical concepts, as well as the role of the teacher in developing meaningful, appropriate tasks with manipulatives.

With those recommendations in mind, imagine the following scenario:

It is the beginning of the year and you are interested in assessing your fourth-grade students' knowledge of place value with large numbers. You ask your students to use a place-value mat and digit cards to show numbers of varying size, with values ranging from single digits up to the hundred thousands. As you state "two thousand one hundred forty-three," you observe your students placing the digits 2, 1, 4, and 3 on their mats. Most of the students don't seem to have too much difficulty placing the digits in the right place to create the desired number. So, it would seem, they have a pretty good handle on the value of larger numbers.

Next, you ask your students to pull out the base ten blocks, with which most, if not all, of the students are familiar. You explain to the students that they are now going to build some numbers with the blocks. Again, you ask them to build numbers of varying values, through the thousands, with the small unit cube representing one and the large cube representing one thousand (see Figure 2–1).

After circulating and jotting down some notes, you seem satisfied with your assessment of each child's ability and are ready to begin the day's lesson of building larger numbers. However, just as you are about to redirect your students, one of them asks, "Don't you want us to build a really big number?" You pause, wondering if you should go ahead with the focus lesson or let the kids jump right into the concept while they're excited about it. You decide to forego the focus lesson for now and pose this challenge to your students: "Yes, I would like for you to build a really big number. We have only the blocks in front of us. How could we use those to build a really big number? Work with your table group and see if you can think of a way to show the number ten thousand."

The students start discussing and quickly come to the realization that they could put ten large cubes together to represent ten thousand. You direct them to study the form of the ten large cubes that they stacked together.

One student says, "It looks like a ten rod, only bigger."

"OK," you continue, "now think of how you might show the number one hundred thousand."

After discussing in their groups for a few minutes, one group of students turn to the table next to them and ask if they could put their thousands cubes together with the other group's. They begin laying large cubes next to each other. Some group members

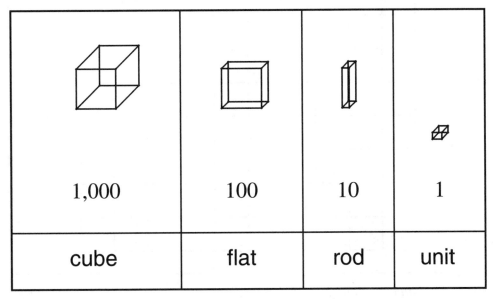

1,000	100	10	1
cube	flat	rod	unit

Figure 2–1 *Base ten blocks*

go off to another table to see if they, too, would like to contribute their large cubes to the effort. Soon, the whole class has congregated into one group, observing as students place together as many large cubes as they can. You ask them to explain what they're doing.

A student turns and replies, "We are putting together one hundred large cubes to make one hundred thousand."

"Why?" you ask.

Another student answers, "Because each cube is worth one thousand, so if we put one hundred together, we will have one hundred thousand."

After working for a few more minutes, they have used as many large cubes as they have (about seventy-five), creating something that resembles a giant partially eaten cracker (see Figure 2–2).

Frustrated, one student says, "But we need more blocks!"

"You do?" you ask. "How many more do you need?"

"We need one hundred cubes all together to show one hundred thousand because each cube is worth one thousand."

"OK. Since we don't have any more large cubes, can you imagine what shape would be formed if you did put one hundred large cubes together?" you ask them.

"I think it will look like a really big hundreds flat," says one student.

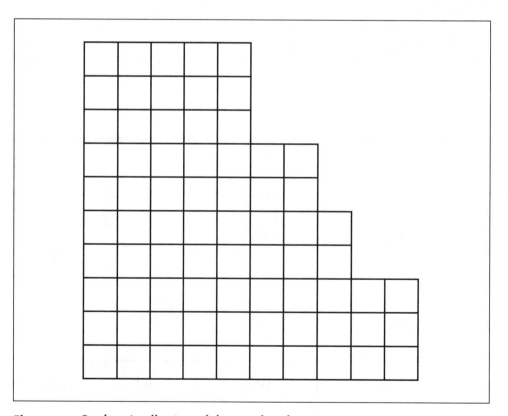

Figure 2–2 *Students' collection of thousands cubes*

You decide that it is a good point to pull the students back for a moment to start making some connections. As they create a large semicircle around the partially constructed one hundred thousand flat, you lay, from right to left, a unit cube, a rod, a flat, and a thousands cube. You ask the students what would come next, and they correctly respond that the "big ten rod" made out of the thousands cubes would come next. Borrowing ten large cubes from the one hundred thousand flat, you lay those end to end in the form of a rod. The kids now have in front of them representations of one through one hundred thousand (at least in part).

You ask them what they notice, and someone says, "This little ones cube is really small compared to the one hundred thousand flat."

Someone else notices that it would take ten of the ten thousand rods to make a one hundred thousand flat.

Another student says, "I notice a pattern: it goes cube, rod, flat, cube, rod, flat."

"OK. So what do you think would come next in this pattern?"

"A really, really big cube!" one student says excitedly.

"And what would be the value of that cube?"

After a moment, one student shouts out, "One million!"

Pushing further, you ask, "How many thousands cubes would we need to build a millions cube? Think about it for a minute and then go to your seat and write about it."

This lesson, which went on perhaps a little longer than you had planned, has proved to be an incredibly powerful way of helping students understand the size and value of larger numbers. By using base ten manipulatives to represent numbers, students were able to construct their own understanding of how numbers grow in value and size, even noticing a pattern that grows exponentially. It's not hard to imagine that those students will carry the image of that large one hundred thousand flat with them as they continue to grow in their understanding of larger numbers.

To help students become more flexible in their thinking, change up which block represents one. In the previous scenario, the small unit cube represented one. Let's say that we do a lesson in which the small cube represents ten. What would the rod represent? (one hundred) Why? What would the flat represent? (one thousand) Why? What would one have to look like? How do you know? These are questions we can ask our students as we encourage them to think differently and to consider the different values of the numbers represented by the blocks.

Base ten blocks are useful for helping students understand larger numbers, but they can also be used to represent smaller numbers. When investigating decimals, another block can represent one, such as the rod. What would the small cube represent? (one-tenth) Why? (because the one is broken into ten equal parts, so each part is called one-tenth) How could we write that? If the flat is one, then a rod is one-tenth and a unit cube is one–one hundredth, and so on. One-thousandth chips are available to continue place value to the thousandths. Again, to help develop students' ability to think flexibly, change up which block is worth one each day: one day it can be the rod, the next day it can be the large cube. The students then must determine the value that the other blocks represent, as shown in Figure 2–3.

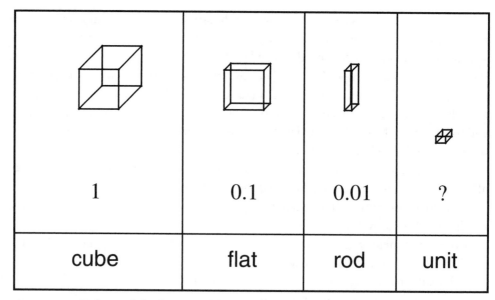

1	0.1	0.01	?
cube	flat	rod	unit

Figure 2–3 *Values of the base ten blocks when the large cube represents one*

Building Understanding Through the Use of Manipulatives

When students can see and manipulate ideas, as illustrated in the previous section, they gain a better understanding of those ideas. Consider the relationship between multiplication and division in this problem:

Daniel's cat had 6 kittens. He sold each kitten for the same amount. He made a total of $54 from selling the kittens. For how much did he sell each kitten?

If students have a manipulative such as counters, they can solve this problem in more than one way. They might group fifty-four counters to represent the total dollar amount earned, and then start giving one dollar to each of six groups until all the money is distributed. In this case, the students have used division to solve the problem: they took the total money amount and *fair shared* it among six groups (see Figure 2–4).

Another student might approach this problem using a guess-and-check strategy. Starting with what she knew (six times five equals thirty), she could experiment with adding two, three, or more counters to each group until the total number of counters reached fifty-four. Finally, after several trials and errors, she would state that six groups of nine equal fifty-four, and therefore each kitten sold for nine dollars.

By sharing out their strategies, students will see that they can solve this problem using division or multiplication and they will begin to see the relationship between the two. Manipulatives help with this discovery by allowing students to experiment with different problem-solving strategies while not being overly concerned with what the "correct" approach might be (read more about this in Chapter 4).

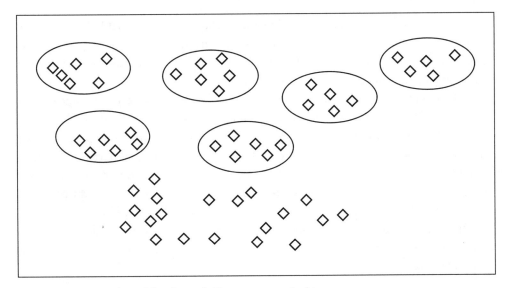

Figure 2–4 *Dividing fifty-four dollars among six kittens*

When our students are learning about naming fractions, we should allow them to explore the concept with different models. We can give them a set of fraction circles or squares (or both) and the direction to find all the different ways to show one-half. Students will begin to see that in each case, although fractions named one-half may not look the same, they cover the same area of the whole (in this case, one part out of two equal parts). One-half of a circle looks different from one-half of a square, and yet we call them both one-half. We can also ask students to use a set of two-color counters or a number line model to demonstrate one-half, as seen in Figure 2–5. Using a model helps reinforce the concept that fractions show *relationships* between a whole and its parts.

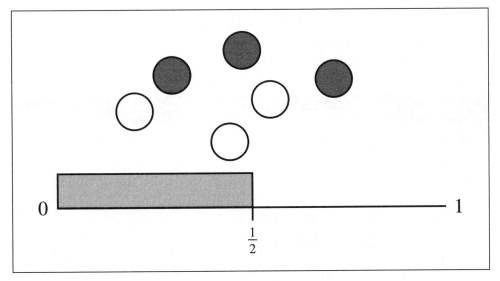

Figure 2–5 *Different representations of one-half*

In each of the representations in Figure 2–5, children can see that half (one of two equal parts or groups) of each whole is shaded, and that while each representation differs from the others in form and area, they all show the same relationship of parts to the whole, and therefore each is called one-half.

When exploring equivalent fractions, it is useful to use one type of manipulative at a time, such as fraction circles or fraction squares. Ask children to build as many equivalent fractions as they can. Their representations would have the same area, but they would look different: one-half would be one out of two equal parts; two-fourths would be two out of four equal parts; three-sixths would be three out of six equal parts; and so on. While the equivalent fractions will look different (because of different-size parts), they will cover the same area because the whole is the same in each case.

There are three models of fractions with which we want our students to be familiar and comfortable using: area/region, length/measurement, and set. Consider the following task:

> **Choose a fraction model (area/region, length/measurement, or set) to represent each of the following situations.** *Explain why you chose the model you did.*
>
> ■ Beth's plant is $3\frac{1}{4}$ inches tall. Judy's plant is twice as tall. How tall is Judy's plant? [length/measurement model]
>
> ■ **Braddock Elementary's fifth-grade classes are planting a vegetable garden. They decide to use $\frac{1}{3}$ of the garden to grow tomatoes. In $\frac{1}{4}$ of the garden, they will grow corn, and in another fourth they will grow beans. In the remaining section they will grow herbs. Show what their garden looks like. What fraction of the garden will be planted with herbs?** [area/region model]
>
> ■ **Mr. Kasik's students are on their way to lunch. There are 24 students in the class. $\frac{1}{3}$ of the children brought their lunch from home, $\frac{1}{2}$ of the children are buying their lunch, and the remaining students are absent. What fraction of the class is absent today?**

Each of these situations can be best represented by a particular fraction model. We want our students to be experienced enough with the different models that they can correctly choose the best representation for a fraction situation.

CLASSROOM-TESTED TIP

Work fractions and percents into your everyday language. After giving whole-group instructions, look for table groups to be ready and describe their representation in different ways:

■ I see one-fourth of James' table is ready.

■ Vincent's table is 33 percent away from being ready.

■ 100 percent of Gabriela's table is ready!

Moving from the Concrete to the Abstract

In geometry, manipulatives are particularly useful as students begin to explore polygons and solids and to classify them according to attributes, as seen in this task:

> **Sort your polygon tiles according to different attributes, and give each group labels. You and your partners should be ready to explain why you sorted them the way you did. Could you have sorted them in a different way? Could some polygons have fit in more than one group? Record your groups on paper by tracing the polygon tiles.**

By allowing students to conduct this investigation with manipulatives (in this case, polygon tiles), we give students the ability to see and feel the different attributes of each tile, and they have the flexibility to move tiles in and out of groups until they are satisfied with their groupings. In addition, by asking them to record their work, we are helping students move from the concrete to the abstract. This is an important step in students' growth as young mathematicians. By being able to work with manipulatives and then create paper-and-pencil representations of their work, students begin to create pictures in their minds, from which they will draw as they are presented with more and more difficult tasks. (See Figure 2–6.)

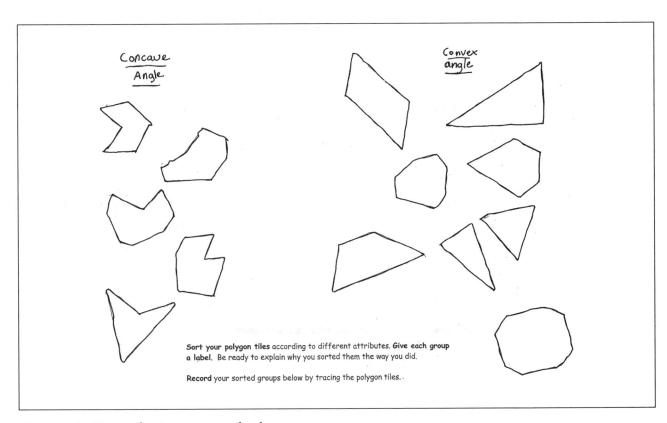

Figure 2–6 *One student's grouping of polygons*

A concept that can be difficult for students is symmetry. How many times do we give students a picture and say, "Draw the lines of symmetry"? By manipulating tiles, pattern blocks, and other objects, students can explore the concept of symmetry in an engaging way, as seen in the following task:

> **Use your color tiles [or tangrams, pattern blocks, etc.] to design a figure that shows symmetry. Sketch your figure on the page below. Draw a line (or lines) to show the line(s) of symmetry. [See Figure 2–7.]**

Again, students are asked to complete a task using concrete materials and then they must move toward a more abstract representation of the concept. As Marzano et al. (2001) point out, the very act of creating a model of the knowledge enhances student understanding of a concept.

Manipulatives and Student Learning Styles

Research shows that humans better retain that which they do, rather than that which they hear or see. In other words, when students are actively, hands-on engaged with their learning, we can feel confident that they are creating more long-term knowledge and understandings than if they experienced concepts passively. Generally speaking, there are six identified learning styles:

■ *Auditory:* Students with this strength are able to recall what they hear and usually prefer oral instructions. They enjoy talking and interviewing, giving oral reports, and listening to recorded books.

■ *Visual:* Students with this learning style are able to recall what they see and prefer written instructions. They learn by observing and enjoy computer graphics, graphs, charts, diagrams, graphic organizers, and text with many pictures.

■ *Tactile:* Students who are tactile learners learn best by touching. They learn best through the use of manipulatives. They enjoy drawing, making models, and following instructions to make something.

■ *Kinesthetic:* Students with this strength learn by touching or manipulating objects. They need to involve their bodies in learning. They enjoy playing games that

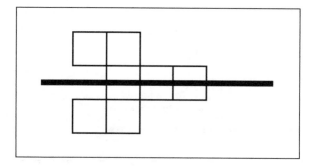

Figure 2-7 *Example figure showing symmetry*

involve their whole body, movement activities, making models, and following instructions to make something.

■ *Global:* These learners do not like to be bored. They learn best when information is presented in an interesting manner using attractive materials. Cooperative learning strategies work well with these students. They enjoy computer programs, games, and group activities.

■ *Analytical:* Students with this learning style like to plan and organize their work. They focus on details and are logical. They learn best when goals are clear, requirements are spelled out, and information is presented in sequential steps.

Using manipulatives and other forms of representation appeals to at least five of these learning styles: visual, tactile, kinesthetic, global, and analytical. Visual learners will benefit from seeing and creating models, diagrams, pictures, and other forms of representation as they experience mathematical concepts. Tactile and kinesthetic learners will appreciate being able to touch manipulatives and use them to make models of the mathematical concepts they are learning. Students with a global learning style will enjoy using virtual manipulatives on the computer, participating in group activities that require the use of concrete manipulatives, and being actively engaged as they create their own understandings of math concepts. Finally, analytical learners enjoy planning and organizing their work, so they will apply logic to their use of materials as they work to solve mathematical problems.

As we become more cognizant of the different ways in which students learn, we can feel confident that by using manipulatives and other representations we are reaching a majority of our students and tapping into their strengths. Students will be more likely to create lasting understandings of concepts if they learn them in hands-on, active ways.

CLASSROOM-TESTED TIP

Good Questioning

Asking questions is an essential part of our approach to teaching and assessing. By asking probing questions, we require students to articulate their thoughts and strategies for solving a problem. Try to include open-ended questions such as these:

■ How did you solve it?

■ Why did you solve it that way?

■ Why do you think you're correct?

■ How could you have solved it a different way?

Manipulatives Can Influence Understanding

In their book *Making Sense*, James Hiebert et al. (1997) argue that the tools that students use can result in students constructing different understandings about concepts. Take, for example, multidigit addition and subtraction. Students who have had many experiences with base ten blocks likely see numbers as made up of units of tens and units of ones, and they will be more likely to construct an understanding that involves adding those units together and then making adjustments. For example, a student who sees the different units in a number may add twenty-six plus thirty-seven in this way:

$$26 + 37 \rightarrow 20 + 30 = 50 \rightarrow 6 + 7 = 13 \rightarrow 50 + 13 = 63$$

On the other hand, children who engage in many counting activities and use hundreds boards will more likely see the counting sequence in an addition or subtraction problem:

$$26 + 37 \rightarrow 20 + 10 = 30 \rightarrow 30 + 10 = 40 \rightarrow 40 + 10 = 50 \rightarrow 50 + 6 = 56 \rightarrow 56 + 7 = 63$$

Each student, based on his own constructed understandings, would then develop his own alternative algorithm for the process. Some students may even have difficulty understanding the traditional algorithm because it does not reflect their understandings about numbers. In some cases, it is difficult for students to move from one concept of numbers to another. That is to say, if their early experiences have been with base ten materials, they are likely to have a units view of multidigit numbers, and they may have difficulty using a counting strategy, even with supports such as number lines. The reverse is true of students whose early experiences were with a counting approach to numbers.

The importance of this phenomenon is that teachers must recognize that the tools they select for their students to use will likely affect the understandings they construct. There is no one correct understanding about a concept, so teachers need not be overly concerned with selecting the *right* tool to help develop students' understanding. Rather, they need to be cognizant of the way in which the tools they choose can influence understandings about a concept, and it would be beneficial to have a conversation with colleagues about this topic when deciding which tools to select.

Manipulatives and Technology

Walk into any classroom and you may see many different ways in which students are using representation to help develop their mathematical understanding: manipulatives such as base ten materials or geometric solids; graphic organizers such as Venn diagrams or tables; and more and more, we see students using technology to represent their thinking. Tools such as virtual manipulatives and interactive whiteboards

Collecting Math Tools

At the beginning of the year, send a letter home to parents (see "Practical Classroom Resources" section on the CD) explaining how you use math tools to help their children develop mathematical understandings. Ask them to begin collecting different items that can be incorporated into their children's learning, and describe possible uses, such as the following:

- *Craft sticks* can be used to explore the concepts of vertical, horizontal, parallel, perpendicular, right angle, acute angle, obtuse angle, and so on.

- *Beans* can be used to explore volume and capacity or as counters and markers.

- *Egg cartons* can be used to explore addition, subtraction, multiplication, division, and fractions, and they can be cut down to serve as a ten-frame.

- *Plastic colorful eggs* can be used to explore addition, subtraction, multiplication, division, and fractions.

- *Small plastic figures*, such as dinosaurs or toy cars, can be used to sort, to explore fractions of a set, or as prompts for creating story problems.

- *Coins* can be used to explore money concepts; plus they're less expensive than buying plastic coins.

- *Small, interesting boxes and containers*, such as cosmetics packaging, can be used to explore the properties of solid figures or the concept of volume, and the numbers on them can be used to create math problems.

- *Everyday containers*, such as milk jugs, soda bottles, and water bottles, can be used to explore volume and capacity and serve as visual benchmarks.

- *Single-serve frozen dinner trays* can be used to hold manipulatives such as number cubes and tiles during a lesson.

- *Plastic sealable bags* of various sizes can be used to create small sets of manipulatives.

- *Ribbon and yarn* can be used to explore measurement concepts or to create a number line.

- *Wrapping paper* can be used during measurement problem-solving activities.

Many of these items can be found around the house and most parents would be happy to have the opportunity to contribute to their child's instructional program. Invite parents into the classroom to learn ways in which they can use items at home to support their children's mathematical learning.

are opening up endless possibilities for teachers and students to create meaning about mathematical topics.

Patricia Moyer, Johnna Bolyard, and Mark Spikell, in their article titled, "What Are Virtual Manipulatives?" (2002), establish a definition of virtual manipulatives. They distinguish between "static" and "dynamic" visual representations of concrete manipulatives. Static visual representations are merely pictures on the screen. They resemble concrete manipulatives, but they cannot be acted upon in the same way concrete manipulatives can. For example, a student may see a picture of two sets of base ten blocks and be asked to add them. With concrete manipulatives, she would be able to combine the two sets, exchanging some blocks for others as necessary, resulting in a sum that was represented by one group of the combined blocks. However, with static visual representations, there is no potential for the student to do any manipulating; she is simply looking at a picture, much as she would see in a textbook or on the overhead projector, and she must do the work mentally (or by creating her own representation with blocks or with paper and pencil).

Dynamic visual representations offer teachers and students many of the same opportunities for manipulating as concrete materials do. Students can manipulate polygons or pattern blocks, for example, to illustrate the geometric transformation terms *translation*, *rotation*, and *reflection*. When learning about subtraction with multidigit numbers, students might use a tool, such as a mallet on the virtual manipulative website www.arcytech.org/java/b10blocks, to "break apart" the larger blocks into their smaller components and move them around. The largest online collection of virtual manipulatives can be found at Utah State University's National Library of Virtual Manipulatives (http://nlvm.usu.edu/en/nav/index.html). This website offers teachers and students learning opportunities in the five NCTM strands: number and operations, algebra, geometry, measurement, and data analysis and probability. It includes lesson plans for teachers and ready-made activities for students. One advantage dynamic manipulatives have over concrete materials is that the shortage problem we sometimes face when we're teaching a lesson is eliminated. Online, there is no shortage of blocks or other math tools; students can create a representation using as many pattern blocks as they want without worrying about running out of hexagons, for example, as sometimes happens when we have a class set of manipulatives that we have split into smaller sets for group work.

An interactive whiteboard also offers a different perspective for students when manipulating visual representations. Any virtual manipulative website can be displayed on the large whiteboard and the dynamic visual representations can be engaged and controlled by the user in a way that is easily visible to peers. For example, when learning about measuring angles, a fifth-grade student can rotate a virtual protractor around an angle to determine its measurement. Figure 2–8 shows a third-grade student illustrating a multiplication fact with an array. The classmates in her group were able to sit around her and watch as she created the array, and it provided her with the opportunity to move and be active during the lesson. Interactive whiteboards have many varied uses and provide us with another way to engage our students and represent concepts in an interesting and active way.

Figure 2–8 *A student uses an interactive whiteboard to illustrate a multiplication fact.*

The Role of the Teacher

The teacher's importance when using manipulatives to build understanding cannot be overstated. We are responsible for modeling how to use the manipulatives, asking questions to push understanding, selecting meaningful tasks, and moving students from the concrete to the abstract. It's very important that teachers have a deep understanding of the mathematics they are teaching. How many times have we gone through the motions of teaching a concept without really getting it ourselves? In addition, we need to be able to understand students' thinking, identify misconceptions, and clear up confusions. This can be done only if we thoroughly understand the mathematics we are teaching. Community colleges, online courses, and district-sponsored training provide opportunities for us to enhance our knowledge of mathematics content and therefore improve our efficacy in teaching math.

As part of our beginning-of-the-year procedures and throughout the year, we model the behaviors we expect of our students so that they are safe and successful. Using math manipulatives is no exception. If we want our students to use them as tools and not toys, we must allow them first to discover the possibilities of how they might be used in a supervised way. For example, popular manipulatives for learning about geometry, fractions, and other concepts are pattern blocks. These colorful blocks are so appealing to learners, both younger and older, and offer so many possibilities in terms of designing and patterning, that we would be mistaken to pass them out to students and jump right into a lesson without giving them exploration time first. Students need time to play, if you will, with the items that they will be using later as tools.

It's likely many of us know firsthand what happens when we don't conduct a guided discovery of a math tool: the students are so engaged in playing with the manipulatives, or in the mere temptation of playing with them, that we have to continually stop to redirect them just to get through the lesson! By allowing them a few minutes to satisfy their natural curiosity, we are setting our students up for a more meaningful learning experience. Another way to facilitate this exploration is to leave baskets of the manipulatives out and allow students to handle them when they have free time.

Base ten blocks, another popular math manipulative, reinforce the concept that our number system uses a system of ten. However, we cannot assume that children will immediately recognize and understand the relationship between the blocks. For example, to see that a rod is worth ten because it is made of ten unit cubes, many children will need to actually lay ten units next to a rod to see the equivalency. The same applies to the relationship between the units, rods, and flats. In addition, we must assist children in learning conservation of number; that is to say that a rod is always worth ten (when the unit is worth one), and therefore it is not necessary to count each part of the rod to determine its value every time. These are just some of the critical roles we play when helping students become proficient in using manipulatives to explore a mathematical concept.

Questions for Discussion

1. How can "seeing" ideas through the use of manipulatives help our students in their growing mathematical understandings?

2. What are some ways in which we can help our students move from the concrete to the abstract? Why is this important?

3. How does the use of manipulatives and other representations appeal to the different learning styles of our students?

4. How can the tools we select to use with our students influence their understandings about a concept?

5. What is the role of the teacher in using manipulatives to teach mathematics?

CHAPTER 3

Using Pictures and Diagrams to Represent Mathematical Thinking

Students who represent the problem in some way are more likely to see important relationships than those who consider the problem without a representation.

— National Council of Teachers of Mathematics,
Principles and Standards for School Mathematics

Student use of manipulatives is essential in developing the conceptual understanding of the mathematics at hand, so it isn't an instructional strategy that should be treated lightly. However, as students move toward more abstract thinking, we need to increase their confidence and abilities in using alternative methods of bringing meaning to their math. As the mathematics becomes more complex, students may find the manipulatives are less helpful, and by necessity they need to rely more on representations that make the problem-solving process more efficient. For this reason, it is important that the representation stage be introduced and modeled while the manipulatives are still on the desk. This allows students an opportunity to make the connection between the two. We must remember that the pictorial representations will have meaning for students only if they have a deep understanding and mastery of the purpose and use of the concrete representations. Research by Piaget confirms the necessity of moving students through these stages, not skipping over them. We need to help students build the bridge between the two. In this chapter we focus on some specific uses for pictures and diagrams as ways to represent the mathematics and look at how students can use those representations to communicate their solutions.

Moving from Manipulatives to Pictures: Why Transition?

Students in grades 3 through 5 move through several mathematical stages in these three years. They begin building and refining their skills with whole-number operations and number relationships and advance to concepts and operations using fractions, decimals, and percents by the end of fifth grade. While certain manipulatives may be useful with whole-number operations of manageable size, they become increasingly cumbersome and sometimes downright difficult, if not impossible, to manage with larger and more complex numbers. When working with complex numbers such as decimals, numbers in the thousands and millions, and/or fractions, students have a choice of trying to make the problem easier by using smaller, more manageable numbers so they can still use the manipulatives or using some type of pictorial or graphic representation that can be applied to the situation and thereby allow them to represent and solve the problem as it is written. Either method will work. Teachers need to model both processes so that students become proficient in working with complex numbers in problem-solving situations.

The type of representations that students choose to use can vary widely. For this reason it is important to allow them the freedom to invent a representation that is meaningful for them. Some students may need to draw realistic pictures to help in solving the problem, but as numbers become more complex, student representations may by necessity become more iconic. Many times, students initially choose to painstakingly draw representations to help them visualize the problem that are so realistic that they spend all of their time drawing pictures and they lose site of the mathematics involved. It's like moving students from Rembrandts to Picassos. Progressing toward more symbolic representations provides students with multiple opportunities to expand their tool kit of strategies when their thinking allows them to make the connections between those symbols and actual shapes.

What Does a Picture Tell You About the Student's Thinking?

A picture *is* worth a thousand words.

Manipulatives are certainly one way to engage students in thinking about the mathematics, and moving from the manipulative stage to the pictorial stage is a natural progression. Pictorial representations provide a more flexible strategy because students can choose how they want to draw a problem. One distinct advantage in allowing students to choose how they want to represent a problem is the thinking it reveals. That thinking may provide clues that some students are not developmentally where they might need to be or where we think they are in their conceptual understanding of the mathematics. In other words, are they trying to solve multidigit computation by picturing the algorithm in their head, or are they trying to make some sense of the numbers that allows them to understand the math?

Have you ever watched in amazement as someone did multidigit computation all in his head? You can almost bet that he wasn't solving a problem such as 345×598

by starting with 8 × 5. There was a lot more going on in his head than going through the steps of the traditional algorithm. The point here is that while students will need to ultimately master the computational algorithm, it is only one strategy, and if we provide our students with only a single strategy for solving computation problems, we are shortchanging them. We need to provide them with classroom experiences that allow them to think about and solve computation problems in a variety of ways. By having students complete pages upon pages of "naked" math computation, you have no sense of their understanding of numbers. Just because students can complete these types of problems does not mean that they can make informed decisions about when to use certain types of computation. Using problems in context and allowing students to choose a representation that demonstrates their understanding of the math will provide much more information than pages of drill.

Consider the following problem:

Micah bought 5 bushels of crabs from the local seafood company. If each bushel contained 41 crabs, how many crabs in all did he buy?

Most students at this level would have no trouble completing this problem computationally using a traditional algorithm. The numbers are manageable and the computation easy, and we would be none the wiser as to what was really going on inside their heads. However, if we ask students to represent this problem pictorially, it is possible to see a little of what they are thinking. In this case (see Figure 3–1) we can see that two students may be at different stages in their conceptual understanding of whole-number multiplication and place value.

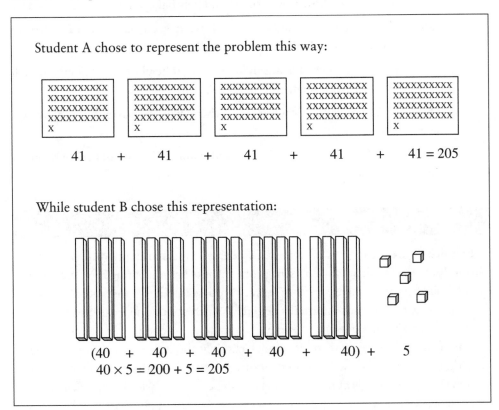

Figure 3–1 *Two different representations of the crab problem*

While both students drew a representation that correctly *matched* the problem, you can begin to see the differences in the way each student thought about the mathematics. Student B seems to have already internalized a crucial concept: ten. By representing the problem using ten rods instead of the individual marks drawn by student A, student B demonstrated an understanding of place value and multiplication that allowed her a more sophisticated sense of the mathematics. While student A represented the problem as repeated addition in his drawing of each complete set, student B began to group like amounts by putting all of the tens together and all of the ones together and then multiplying a manageable benchmark number. Moving students away from counting as a method of computation and toward conceptualizing benchmark numbers such as ten allows students to transition to more complex computation. In this case, student A hadn't demonstrated that skill and needed additional practice with the base ten blocks and benchmark numbers such as ten and one hundred. Counting is an inefficient method of solving computation problems, and students who continue to try to count when solving problems instead of chunking the numbers into meaningful quantities will experience more difficulty when the numbers become more complex.

You cannot see your students' thinking without occasionally having them represent problems pictorially. A representation strategy such as this can be used as an exit ticket or warm-up activity that will allow for a quick and easy informal assessment, providing valuable information. Following are some sample exit ticket problems using pictorial representations:

1. **Margo baked cookies with her mom for the school bake sale. If they put 12 cookies on each pan, how many cookies did they bake in all if they used 5 pans?**

2. **Patty bought 9 bags of candy at the store. If each bag held 22 pieces of candy, how much candy did she have in all?**

3. **Charlie planted 5 rows of beans in his garden. If he planted 18 plants in each row, how many bean plants did he have in all?**

4. **There are 23 students in each class. If there are 12 classes, how many students are there in all?**

5. **Each stack of CDs contains 53 CDs. How many CDs would there be in 24 stacks?**

CLASSROOM-TESTED TIP

Exit tickets are great ways of assessing students' understanding of the daily lesson. By asking students to represent problems just before exiting the classroom and collecting their papers as they leave, you have a reliable method of assessment that can be used to inform the next day's instruction. These can also be used as warm-ups in the same way if you have your students complete them at the beginning of class. Having them do a quick check at the start of class provides you with some instant data on how students are progressing with a particular skill or concept. By doing this at the start of class, you can quickly look over their work and make decisions for that day's lesson or flexible grouping time.

The same type of thinking can be assessed when looking at division. Why is it that our students find division so difficult to master and painful to practice, and why is it that we find ourselves spending so much time teaching and reteaching the skill? Perhaps it is because there are so many steps involved in the process and some of the skills needed for the process may not have been mastered? Maybe, but consider the importance of developing number sense as it applies to division instead of having students continue to practice page after page of division problems without context until they have memorized the steps. And how many of us resort to using those mnemonic devices to help our students remember all of those steps?

*D*ivide, *m*ultiply, *s*ubtract, *c*ompare, *b*ring down: *Does McDonald's serve cheeseburgers?*

Instead of focusing on having students memorize the steps, let's take a look at what manipulatives and representations can be used to help them really learn and understand the mathematics and how students can be encouraged to share their thinking through representation.

Place value is an often overlooked part of the division process. We sometimes become so concerned with what goes into what that we confuse students with our models and language. After giving students a problem such as 324 ÷ 2, you might ask, "How many times does two go into three?" How many of our students have the understanding that the three is really three hundreds? We assume they are looking at the problem correctly, but is this really the case? Perhaps it is time to pull out the base ten blocks and model a few problems, making sure that your language concerning place value and the division situation is consistent with the mathematics. Once students have practiced the process a few times, help students begin to see how they can record their solutions graphically.

While base ten blocks are certainly not the only manipulative that can be useful in this situation, keep in mind that as the numbers increase in value, individual counters become unwieldy and encourage counting. Using base ten blocks makes it more likely that students will begin to move away from counting and rely more on understanding the value of the numbers involved in the problem. Try modeling this entire problem (324 ÷ 2) without even using the words *divide* and *goes into*. You might instead use words such as *exchange*, *trade*, or *share*.

Ms. Malone presented her fourth-grade class with the following problem and asked students to model and record their steps pictorially instead of doing the traditional algorithm.

Kelly had 324 pieces of chocolate. If she had an equal number of dark chocolate and milk chocolate pieces, how many of each did she have?

Daniel set his problem up as in Figure 3–2.

Daniel explained his solution this way: He began by sharing out the two hundred flats (one each for the milk chocolate and dark chocolate), and then since he had only one hundred left, he needed to exchange or trade the third hundred flat for ten rods, giving him a total of twelve rods. With an even number of rods, Daniel was able to

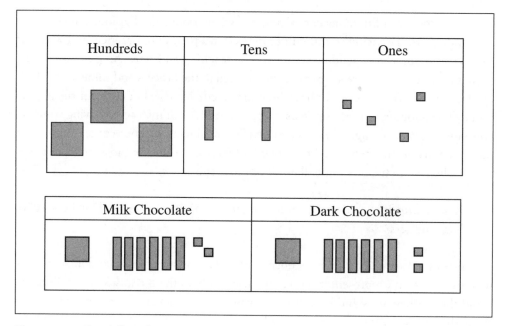

Hundreds	Tens	Ones

Milk Chocolate	Dark Chocolate

Figure 3–2 *Daniel's solution*

share the twelve rods, giving each type of chocolate six rods. The four final pieces were evenly shared out at two each. His final solution showed that there was an equal share for the dark chocolate and the milk chocolate with no chocolate remaining. Ms. Malone asked Daniel if there were any clues in the problem that there would be no remainder and he responded that since he was making only two groups and the number 324 ended in an even number, he knew there would be no remainder.

It is important at this stage not to worry too much about the traditional algorithm. This is certainly something that is easier said than done, but consider how much instructional time we have spent practicing the algorithm only to have to start all over again once the problems increase to two-digit divisors. The focus has to be on helping students make the conceptual connection between the concrete manipulative, the symbolic representation, and ultimately the process. Once that connection is made, the algorithm can be introduced alongside the representation. Students may in fact find their own ways of showing the numeric representation that makes sense to them. Drawing the base ten shapes may be too time-consuming, so it's OK for them to invent their own representations.

At this stage, the teacher might wonder whether Daniel could actually do the traditional representation. Chances are good that he could, but she at least would have a clear picture of how Daniel was thinking when it came to division. If the teacher continued with the base ten models or the representation of the models, division problems involving interpretation of remainders would make more sense. Students working with the following situation would have a better grasp of the meaning of the numbers if they were working with some type of representation instead of only the numbers.

137 students from Delmar Elementary are going on a field trip to the Baltimore Zoo. If each of the buses seats 35 students, how many buses will be needed?

In this problem we have advanced to a two-digit divisor, but representing the 137 students using a model of base ten does not require students to represent each individual student. Who wants to make 137 *X*'s across her paper or count out 137 counters? Being able to represent the one hundred using one flat or ten rods makes the problem more manageable and contributes to the understanding of place value. We want our students to view this problem in terms of one hundred or thirteen tens, not simply one hundred thirty-nine ones. Remember: benchmark numbers are key to student understanding of more complex problems. Students working through this problem would begin by taking the thirteen rods and putting them in groups of thirty since the buses each hold thirty-five students. Then they would exchange the final rod for ten units, giving them seventeen units to share among the four buses. Some students may even be able to correctly determine the number of buses without sharing the seventeen units since seventeen is less than four buses times five remaining seats. Could they do that without representing the problem symbolically? Maybe, but there is no doubt that representing the problem symbolically offers a powerful look at what the problem truly means.

The important thing to remember here is not to rush the use of the algorithm. Until students have that deep conceptual understanding of the division process as it relates to place value, memorizing the steps in the process will not lead to long-term retention of the skill. The goal is to provide students with an understanding that they can translate to more complex numbers. Without that understanding, division just becomes a series of "What goes into what?" questions. Following are a few sample division problems in context that students can represent pictorially:

1. The circus sold 124 tickets to ride an elephant around the ring before the show. If the elephant could carry 5 children at a time, how many rides did the elephant make?

2. Lightbulbs come in packages of 4. How many packages would be needed for 212 lightbulbs?

3. The flower shop had 85 roses. If there were 5 vases, how many flowers were in each vase?

4. At the carnival 6 tickets are needed to ride the Ferris wheel. If 324 tickets were collected one evening, how many people rode the Ferris wheel?

Can You Really Teach Fractions so They Will Remember? Absolutely!

All math teachers have at times struggled with teaching fractional concepts and operations, and just as many teachers have been frustrated to the point of throwing their hands up in the air in surrender when their students just don't get it. Why is it that our students don't seem to be able to retain fractional concepts from one year to the next or even one day to the next? Does it matter? How many times in your adult life have you had to divide fractions or add six-elevenths and six–twenty-thirds? Let's face it: fractions hold little or no meaning for our students, they seldom see them or use them in real life, and their only exposure to fractions seems to be in the math classroom. As teachers, we even struggle to find real-life applications for fractional use beyond dividing a pizza or doubling a recipe! But wait, before you throw the fractions out the window, remember that fractions are not just about adding, subtracting, multiplying, dividing, and don't forget the ever popular "reducing to lowest terms" types of problems. Fractions are found in a multitude of other contexts, such as probability, ratios and proportions, measurement, and later on, scale factor. It is for this reason we need to spend additional time helping students internalize fraction concepts and, yes, continue to develop the ever elusive number sense as it applies to fractions.

Typically, teachers spend little instructional time developing the concept of what a fraction is or how big or small it is before moving headlong into teaching computational skills. After all, there is a lot of curriculum to cover! Spending more time helping students internalize what a fraction is and what characteristics it has may lead to needing less time to teach computation skills. Using manipulatives long enough for students to conceptualize some of the basic benchmark terms such as *halves*, *thirds*, and *fourths* is important, and it isn't enough for the teacher to model the fractions; the manipulatives need to be in students' hands. There, we said it again: the manipulatives need to be in students' hands.

There are a number of commercially produced manipulatives that can be used with fraction instruction. Pattern blocks are great for helping students see the relationship of part to whole. Using the yellow hexagon as the whole, students can clearly see that the green triangle is one-sixth of the whole while the red trapezoid is one-half. What happens when the trapezoid becomes the whole? What fraction does the triangle represent now? When the triangle becomes the whole, how do you describe the parallelogram or the hexagon?

However, as with many other concepts and processes in mathematics, fractions are another example of where the manipulatives will go only so far. Keep in mind that the goal is to move students toward a more symbolic phase of representation, whether real or invented. It doesn't matter how the representation is drawn as long as it makes the math more meaningful for the student.

Take Your Cue from Reading Instruction

Look in any good reading manual and you will see a great deal of importance is placed on getting students ready to read. Building background knowledge is one of the key components in reading instruction. Its purpose is to increase the likelihood that a student will not only be interested in but also understand what he is about to read. It is no different with math. We need to actively build on what students already know and can do. Regardless of the grade level and content, activating prior knowledge is essential to bringing meaning to new concepts. Brain research indicates that when new information is being introduced, students are trying to connect it with what they already know. Isn't that how we all approach new knowledge? Many students do not see math around them on a daily basis, and unlike reading, they seldom go home at night and solve math problems for pleasure. They don't realize how math impacts their lives, so it becomes important for us to find ways to make the math meaningful to them and connect it to their world.

Before: Activate prior knowledge

Jump-start your students' thinking! Fractions are not just about pizza and dividing rectangles, and yet most of us learned fractions in that context. Before starting instruction on a new concept or skill, take the time to find out what the children already know about fractions and how they think about them. One way to do this is to engage students in a freewriting activity. It is more like a freewriting and drawing activity, but it allows students to demonstrate their understandings or misunderstandings where fractions are concerned. Students in Mrs. Harbinson's fifth-grade class regularly engage in writing activities prior to learning new concepts and skills. Before the unit on fractions, she had them begin with a blank sheet of paper and she asked them to represent or describe as many fractional concepts and skills as they could. By encouraging them to use not only words and numbers but pictures and diagrams, she was able to see how some of them visualized the concepts. Seeing students use nonlinguistic forms of representations to illustrate fractional terms and processes can be very insightful for a classroom teacher. For example, one student in the class represented thirds, and while she divided a circle and a rectangle into three sections and shaded in one section, she didn't attempt to make the three parts appear equal.

Occasionally you may find that you see work similar to that in Figure 3–3. While this example certainly shows several ways to look at three-fourths, there are a lot of missing pieces. Are those pieces missing because the student did not yet have mastery of those skills or did she just decide not to include them? The work does demonstrate the relationship that fractions have as a part of a set and a part of the whole, and the student included appropriate vocabulary. When vocabulary is present, the teacher needs to look for how it is used and in what context. We can also see in this representation that there was an understanding of the size of the fraction as it relates to one-half and one by placing it on the number line or ruler between the two numbers. There isn't much to analyze especially as it might relate to operations with fractions, but as a teacher, Mrs. Harbinson now knew that there was a lot of information to build on and nothing that seemed to need reteaching. Looking at student work, teachers need to ask questions such as Are the students able to represent fractions as not only parts of a whole but also parts of a set? Are there illustrations that represent numerators, denominators, or mixed numbers? Do the students have a beginning understanding of any of the computational processes as they involve fractions? It is amazing the thinking and the prior knowledge that can be seen in student work of this nature.

Jump-starting their thinking might also mean finding unique and interesting applications for the concept. For example, Mr. Alston's fifth-grade class is studying Egyptian history. As a way of getting students more interested in the upcoming unit on fractions, he showed his students how the Egyptians represented fractions. To make the lesson more realistic, he had the students create papyrus scrolls for their work

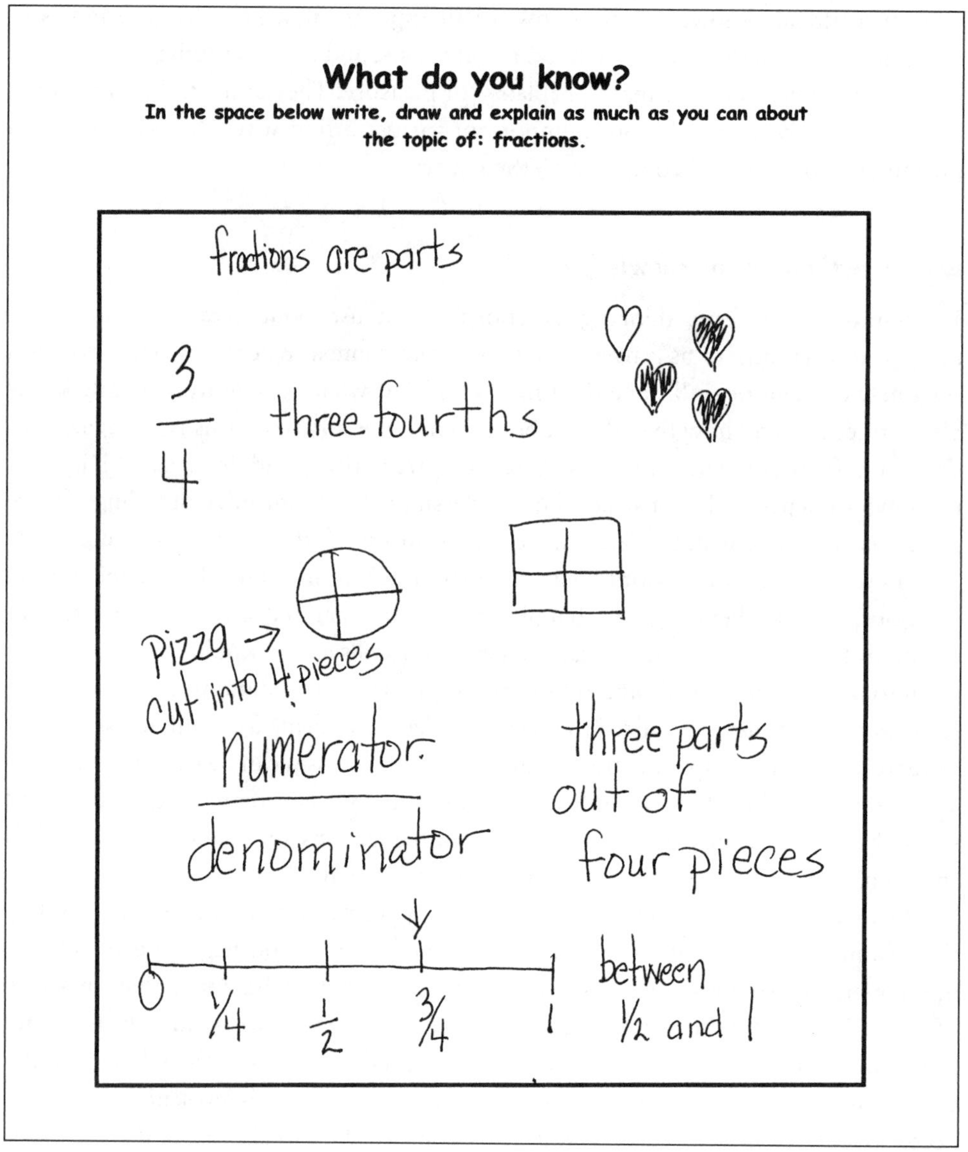

What do you know?
In the space below write, draw and explain as much as you can about
the topic of: fractions.

$\frac{3}{4}$ three fourths

fractions are parts

Pizza → cut into 4 pieces

$\frac{numerator}{denominator}$

three parts out of four pieces

between ½ and 1

0   ¼   ½   ¾   1

Figure 3-3 *One student's ideas about fractions*

area as he presented an Egyptian math lesson. Mr. Alston explained that the Egyptians used only fractions with a numerator of one, called unit fractions. Marie immediately raised her hand and said, "That would make it a lot easier to compare fractions if the numerator is always one, since you only have to look at the denominator."

Mike, on the other hand, asked, "If they only used fractions with numerators of one, how did they write a fraction like three-fourths?" The class began offering ideas such as adding one-fourth three times to get to three-fourths and just when they thought they had it figured out, Mr. Alston gave them another important fact. He told them that when the Egyptians wanted to represent a fraction such as three-fourths, they did indeed put unit fractions together, but they were not allowed to use the same fraction more than once when they did this. Needless to say, everyone thought the situation was hopeless and the Egyptians had "funny rules for math." Since students already had experience in adding fractions with unlike denominators, Mr. Alston challenged them to find a solution to the three-fourths dilemma.

Students took out their dry-erase boards and set to work looking for a solution. Mike's group found the answer first and proudly displayed it: $\frac{1}{2} + \frac{1}{4} = \frac{3}{4}$. Could other fractions be rewritten as sums of unit fractions as well? The excitement that this type of activity generated not only helped the students prepare for the upcoming unit but also helped them remember some of the skills and concepts from previous instruction on fractions. The students were excited about the challenge of representing fractions as sums of a unit and even set out to draw pictures to go along with their computations. The "Resources for Teachers" section of this book lists some excellent websites with information on this topic.

Another way prior knowledge can be activated and new knowledge presented is using a strategy called concept formation or concept attainment. This strategy provides students with an opportunity to build on what they already know about a specific topic while refining and clarifying the concept's specific characteristics. Using a chart similar to the one in Figure 3–4, you need to provide students with examples and nonexamples of the concept or skill you are trying to develop or extend (see CD for a blank chart). At the same time, it is important to make a conscious effort to avoid calling that concept by name. The purpose of this activity is to get students to describe, not name, the concept or skill.

Figure 3–4 is an example of one of the benchmark fractions, one-fourth. In this case we are representing the fraction as both a fractional part of a set and a fractional part of a whole. Depending on where students are in their skill development, examples might need to be limited to one or the other. As students study the chart and the examples, ask key questions such as, "What do the examples have in common?" and "How do the nonexamples differ?" As students respond, encourage them to describe the characteristics of the examples and at the same time be specific about why the nonexamples are nonexamples. One sample student response might be "In the top row, each column has one smiley face shaded in, but the example has four faces and the nonexample has only three faces." Allow students to continue verbalizing the characteristics, and when they think they know what the concept is, prompt them to create their own examples and nonexamples. A note of caution: Make sure students aren't just drawing a different shape and mimicking each example in quantity and shading.

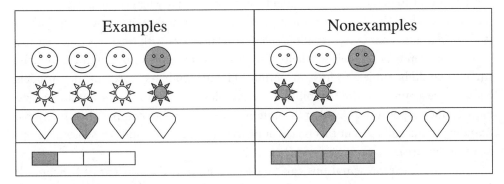

Figure 3–4 *Chart used for concept formation*

Not all students will be as quick to reach a conclusion about the concept as others. For that reason, having students draw their own examples allows them to continue to be engaged while giving the rest of the students additional time to continue thinking about the similarities and differences found in the examples and nonexamples.

For students in grades 3 through 5 this particular concept should already be a part of their working knowledge, but it is still important to take time to activate that prior knowledge no matter what the skill is, by using key questions to get students thinking about a specific topic. You never know what misconceptions might be uncovered. Occasional informal assessments such as this activity work great with dry-erase boards as a quick check or as a precursor to introducing equivalent or more complex fractions and mixed numbers.

We can also activate prior knowledge using manipulatives. In the last chapter, we described how to use two-color counters to help develop the concept of fractional parts of a set where the whole was represented by the total number of counters and each color became a part of the set. Activities such as this help students model the concepts, but unless your classroom has an unlimited budget for manipulatives (and ours doesn't), you have to move from the concrete manipulative to student representations to continue to illustrate this concept. In essence you are building the bridge that will connect the concrete to the symbolic representation. It also allows for more flexibility when you have your students draw something other than counters or tiles.

During: on to the new material

Look in almost any mathematics textbook at this level and you will surely find problems requiring students to put four or five fractions in order from least to greatest. What strategy do we use? Most textbooks will provide examples where students are asked to find common denominators for all of the fractions before putting them in order. Computationally this makes the end result easier to determine, but what does it tell us about the student's abilities to understand the magnitude of the numbers? Keep in mind, if the purpose of putting fractions in order of least to greatest is to assess student understanding of the size of a given fraction and its relationship to other fractions, can we assess that accurately if we provide them with a computation model that they only have to replicate over and over again?

One way for students to compare fractions with one another without having to find a common denominator is to compare them first with the benchmark fractions. It is important to make sure that students understand that when comparing fractions with one another, the whole unit must be the same. It is also necessary to point out to students that they cannot use the same rules for relative size with fractions that they use with whole numbers. Models will help with this concept, but without multiple models, students could be subject to misconceptions. Having students represent their models allows once again for more flexibility. Fraction tiles or fraction circles should be used initially; they support the idea that the unit must be the same to compare two fractions. Avoiding tricks and rules at this phase of process is crucial for number sense development in this area.

Number line representations can be used to support the concept of benchmark fractions and if the number lines are identical, the idea of same-size unit is reinforced.

A student asked to compare the fractions three-fifths and four-ninths might draw a representation similar to the one in Figure 3–5.

The relationship these two fractions have to one-half allows the student to first compare them separately with one-half and then compare them with each other. Because three-fifths is greater than one-half and four-ninths is less than one-half, three-fifths is greater than four-ninths. Using one number line for this skill might confuse students just beginning this process, so it might be more helpful to keep the number lines separate at first. Ultimately, students should reach a point where they can show the two fractions on one line, but initially they may have to divide each number line into appropriate sections before comparing. In addition to comparing fractions with one-half, the number line can also be used for other benchmarks. Students might be asked to determine how far from one each number is or which number is closer to zero. Every time students engage in an activity such as this, they are thinking about the size of the fraction and its relationship to the unit. They aren't trying to memorize steps in finding the least common multiple and then comparing numerators.

Comparing numerators when the denominators are the same is certainly a strategy for ordering fractions, as is comparing denominators when the numerators are identical, but if used in isolation this practice may cause students to apply whole-number concepts to the fractions at other times. One way to keep student thinking in check is to get students to represent their fractions pictorially. Then you can clearly see how they are looking at the fractions in relationship to one another.

After: been there, done that—moving on!

Don't you just love it when a student says, "Why are we doing this? We learned that in the last chapter," and "We've already taken the test," or "Why are we doing a geometry problem when we are supposed to be working on division?" Like it or not, that is how most students view mathematics instruction: in isolation. It becomes imperative to continue to spiral back and reassess student thinking as well as help students make connections to the new concepts as we are teaching them. We need to provide students with opportunities to demonstrate the connective nature of the mathematics and extend and refine their thinking as it relates to the more complex processes.

As an example, students can use the same number line used for ordering fractions to order decimals and then order decimals and fractions in combination. Base ten

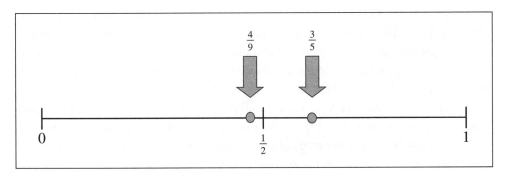

Figure 3–5 *Using a number line to compare fractions*

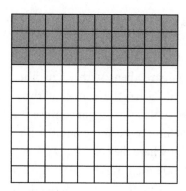

Figure 3–6

blocks and their appropriate representations can now be used to support instruction using decimals. If the one thousand cube now becomes one unit, what does the ten rod become? Decimals, fractions, and percents are often found in isolation in many textbooks; why not combine the representations in order to help students make the connection? Consider the representation in Figure 3–6.

Using a representation such as the one in Figure 3–6, you can ask students if the figure represents $\frac{3}{10}$, 30 percent, or .3. Ask students how many different ways they can represent a certain number or how many names they can find for a certain representation. All of these activities lead to an increase in number sense and an understanding of the connected nature of the mathematics.

The Role of the Teacher

It is important for teachers to provide students with multiple opportunities to interact with concepts and express themselves mathematically so that their thinking is revealed. It doesn't come from pages of drill and kill and it doesn't come from limiting them to one numeric representation. Studies such as TIMSS (Trends in International Mathematics and Science Study) illustrate the need for a change in our approach to mathematics instruction. One such change is in allowing students to work through problem-solving situations either independently or cooperatively and construct meaning from the mathematics without having to be told what math is involved. Students who are allowed to work through problems without first having to memorize steps in an algorithm are much more likely to internalize the mathematics and thus reduce the nearly 53 percent amount of time spent reviewing concepts in an average eighth-grade classroom (Hiebert et al. 2003).

A mathematics class rich in context and problem-solving opportunities is much more likely to yield students ready for more complex situations, and allowing students to use their own representations to illustrate their thinking will help teachers immediately zero in on misconceptions and inefficient strategies.

Figure 3–7 *Provide students with opportunities to represent math ideas.*

Questions for Discussion

1. How can a standards-based classroom be a problem-based classroom?

2. How can the use of representations help students extend and refine their understanding of the mathematics?

3. What connections to the context can students demonstrate with their representations?

4. How can teachers use alternative forms of representations to help jump-start instruction?

4

Using Numbers and Symbols to Represent Mathematical Ideas

Like other forms of written literacy, mathematical representations allow
for visual inspection of work and reduce cognitive demands on memory.

—Sara P. Fisher and Christopher Hartmann, "Math Through the Mind's Eye."

Moving from Pictures to Equations

As we discussed in the previous chapter, pictures are an important way in which children learn to show their mathematical thinking, and the sophistication of their pictorial representations grows developmentally. The leap between pictures and numbers, however, is not an easy one for some students. Moving from the concrete to the abstract requires a deep understanding of a topic, although we might argue that there are plenty of students who can use numbers successfully without having worked in the concrete first. However, when we ask them to explain their thinking in words, or even to go from the abstract of numbers to creating a concrete model of the process they used, we find that there are holes in their understanding and that they are often performing certain procedures automatically without a foundation of real understanding about why those procedures work or what they mean. Our goal, then, is to move students from pictures to equations when they are developmentally ready and to guide them toward more standard numerical representations when appropriate.

In this chapter, we discuss the importance of developing students' understanding of what numbers and symbols mean, and ways in which we can support them in this growth. We also discuss the role of invented algorithms and the use of equations to solve problems and visualize math ideas. Finally, the role of the teacher in this area of student learning is examined.

It's All About Timing

Timing is everything, as they say. If we attempt to move our students from the concrete to the abstract too early, or worse yet, skip the concrete altogether, we'll find ourselves with a group of students who are consumed with remembering formulas and facts without really thinking about the mathematics behind a problem. If they can't recall those algorithms, they'll have absolutely nothing to fall back on. We do a disservice to students when we teach procedures rather than concepts. How many of us learned that the formula for the area of a rectangle is length times width? It's likely that we stored this procedural approach to an area problem in our brain and retrieved it when we thought is was applicable, without creating a visual in our head or on paper that would assist in our understanding of the problem. Similarly, we may have the formula for the perimeter of a rectangle tucked safely away: $2s^1 + 2s^2$. How many times, though, have we seen a student faced with a perimeter problem of an irregular polygon who did not use the understanding that perimeter is the distance *around* something? Rather, he tried to apply the formula for a rectangle to the irregular polygon and froze up when he could not make it work. The student had nothing to fall back on, no mental tool box from which to pull different strategies.

What do numbers really mean? How can we support students' growing understanding of numbers and symbols? These are important questions that we must ask ourselves as we plan meaningful learning experiences for our students. Defining the word *number* is not an easy task in itself. Indeed, one Web inquiry into the definition of the word led us to more than ten separate definitions! It is no wonder that without concrete learning experiences, some students find conventions such as numbers and symbols very difficult to master.

One way in which we can help our students to make the connection between the concrete and the abstract is by using manipulatives or models, linking the process to numbers and symbols, and then weaning them from the manipulatives. Consider this task:

> **What is half of 50? How can this help you to figure out what half of 48 is? Explain your thinking.**

In Figure 4–1, we see a student using small cubes to solve this problem. She made a five-by-ten array and then slid her pencil in the middle to split it into two groups. By observing her work, it was possible to see that she was comfortable using the model of an array and that she understood that finding half of something means splitting it into two equal groups. She then was able to make a record of her work on paper (see Figure 4–2). Although she did not yet know how to write $\frac{1}{2}$ of 50 = 25 symbolically, she could justify it with manipulatives and then create a representation of her thought process on paper. Because she was able to do these things and could communicate her understanding of the concept, she was probably ready to learn the symbols associated with her actions. The timing, in this case, was just right!

Two concepts that are typically introduced in third grade are multiplication and division. Fortunately, the days of simply requiring students to memorize the facts without connecting them to some type of model are behind us. Real understanding of these

Figure 4–1 *A student uses cubes to help solve a problem.*

concepts is developed through manipulating objects in and out of groups before the numbers and symbols associated with the task are ever introduced. In fact, the language we use typically does not follow the symbols in the beginning. We are more likely to say, "How can we show four groups of five?" rather than ask the students what four times five equals. In the following task, students are asked to think about equal groups.

Nora and three of her friends are selling balloons at their school fair. They each are holding five balloons. How many balloons are Nora and her friends holding?

Assuming students have had plenty of opportunity to solve similar tasks using manipulatives such as counters or blocks, we may find the students are ready for pictorial representations. After perhaps sketching a picture of four friends holding five balloons apiece (see Figure 4–3), students may solve the problem by assigning a value to each friend or to each balloon. They may write a five above each group of balloons, or they may write the numbers one through twenty above the balloons, counting them out.

The strategy they choose may show their understanding of the concept of multiplication as equal groups and/or repeated addition. They may even use counting by fives to solve the problem: five, ten, fifteen, twenty. It is not until they have a deep understanding that multiplication *looks like* equal groups (whether it's through a sketch, as seen in Figure 4–3, or as an array) that we should begin to introduce the symbols associated with the problem: $4 \times 5 = 20$.

The same problem can be modified to ask students to think about taking a large group and splitting it equally, or fairly.

What is half of 50?   Show your thinking below.

25   25

How can this help you know what half of 48 is?
Explain your thinking.

I think that if you make forty-eihte
sqwars and put your pencle inside
and count the sqwars on the
left and the rihte then you
can finger out what is half of
48. The anser is 24.

Figure 4–2 *The student made a paper-and-pencil representation of the work she did with blocks.*

Nora and three of her friends are selling balloons at their school fair. They have 20 balloons to sell, and they are each holding the same number of balloons. How many balloons is each of them holding?

Students can use the same approach to solve this problem as with the previous one: they can fair share twenty blocks into four groups, or sketch out groups of balloons until all twenty are used and each group has the same number. Some students may even begin to make the connection that to solve each of these problems, their representations

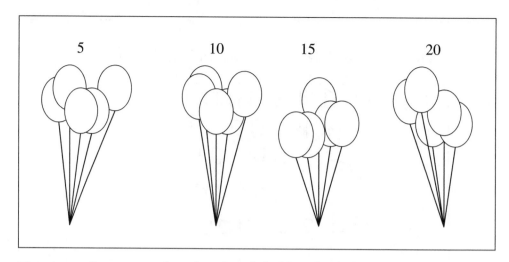

Figure 4–3 *One way to show four friends holding five balloons each*

are similar, if not the same! What a powerful way to help students see the relationship between multiplication and division. When students have these images in their minds of what multiplication and division *look* like, then they are ready to learn the symbolic representation of the operations. Long before multiplication facts are memorized, students search their brains for a representation associated with each fact: an array or their hands or groups of objects. By giving them a lot of practice with developing these representations, we are assisting students in the process of committing their facts to memory.

Decimals are usually introduced in third grade and then the concept is further developed in subsequent grades. Many students' early experience with decimals is through money. They learn the names of the coins, their values, and how to write them using numbers. How many of them, though, can tell us why the value of a penny is written as \$0.01 or a quarter is written as \$0.25? Do they understand what those numbers represent? If they have been taught decimals and fractions simultaneously or at least in close proximity, then perhaps they will make the connection that a penny is written as \$0.01, or one-hundredth, because it is one-hundredth of a dollar. Similarly, a quarter is written as \$0.25 because its value is twenty-five–hundredths of a dollar. It cannot be emphasized enough that students need many experiences with concrete materials before they fully develop an understanding of a concept and what the symbols associated with it mean. With money, they need to handle one hundred pennies to begin to understand the relationships between a penny and a dollar, a half-dollar, a quarter, a dime, and a nickel. Only when they really have an image in their mind about what one-hundredth of a dollar looks like is it the right time to introduce the symbols of money and other decimals. As mentioned in Chapter 2, base ten blocks are wonderful tools for introducing larger numbers as well as smaller ones.

When using base ten blocks to introduce larger and smaller numbers, play a listening game with the kids. Designate which block is worth one (e.g., the small unit cube if working with whole numbers or the large cube if working with fractions or decimals). Drop the blocks, one at a time, on an overhead or table and ask the children to guess the value of the block you dropped. For example, if the small unit cube represents one, then when the kids hear the flat dropped, they will shout out, "One hundred!" This reinforces the size of the different numbers in an aural way in addition to a visual one.

Near the end of a unit on fractions, decimals, and percents, some fifth-grade students were asked to do the following task:

Think about money. Create a chart to show:

■ the fractional part of a dollar represented by each coin

■ the decimal equivalent of each coin

■ the percent value for each coin

■ the coin written as money (e.g., $0.25)

■ a visual to show the value of the coin

Question: How can you use this data to figure out what $\frac{2}{5}$ of one dollar is? $\frac{3}{4}$ of one dollar? $\frac{7}{10}$ of one dollar? Show your thinking.

In Figure 4–4, we can see a sample of one student's work. She was able to show symbolic representations of fractions, decimals, and percents, and she was also able to create a picture of what each coin value looks like. This activity had meaning for her because she had a conceptual understanding of each of those symbols. She wasn't merely writing numbers down based on memorization. Also, she was able to take the information on the chart and apply it, determining what different fractional values of a dollar might be.

The Role of Alternative Algorithms

Alternative, or invented, algorithms are procedures children have invented to help them solve mathematical problems. They are termed *alternative* because they are often idiosyncratic and do not resemble the algorithms that are traditionally associated with operations. *Principles and Standards for School Mathematics* (NCTM 2000) asserts the importance of encouraging students to use written mathematical

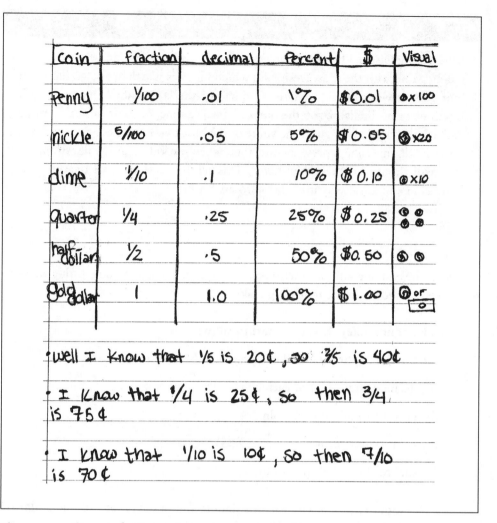

Coin	fraction	decimal	Percent	$	Visual
Penny	1/100	.01	1%	$0.01	⊙ × 100
nickle	5/100	.05	5%	$0.05	⊙ × 20
dime	1/10	.1	10%	$0.10	⊙ × 10
Quarter	1/4	.25	25%	$0.25	⊙ ⊙ ⊙ ⊙
half dollar	1/2	.5	50%	$0.50	⊙ ⊙
gold dollar	1	1.0	100%	$1.00	⊙ or ☐

• well I know that 1/5 is 20¢, so 2/5 is 40¢

• I know that 1/4 is 25¢, so then 3/4 is 75¢

• I know that 1/10 is 10¢, so then 7/10 is 70¢

Figure 4-4 *One student's work on the money problem*

representations to help them make sense, even if those representations are unconventional. For example, the traditional way of solving a two-digit addition problem involves putting down and carrying, or regrouping, as it is commonly termed. A child using an alternative algorithm might use an expanded form to add, as shown in Figure 4–5.

In Figure 4–6, we see how one student solved the same multiplication problem in different ways. For the traditional way of solving the problem, as seen in the solution on the top right-hand side of the paper, the student had to line up the digits correctly and use the zero as a placeholder. For many of us, this was the only way we learned how to multiply larger numbers. Next, she used a partial-product method. She broke out the four different multiplication problems within the two-digit-by-two-digit problem and then added up the products. Finally, she used what some students call the box, or place-value, method. She broke apart each two-digit number, multiplied in the matrix, and then added the partial products. The second and third methods she used to solve the problem show an understanding of place value and process. While she could solve the problem correctly using the traditional method, we don't gain an insight into

Traditional Algorithm	Alternative Algorithm
127 +68 95	27 = 20 + 7 +68 = 60 + 8 80 + 15 = 95

Figure 4–5 *Two ways to solve an addition problem*

her understanding of the problem by looking at that solution. For all we can tell, she has memorized a procedure and applied it. Alternative algorithms often give us insight into a child's understanding (or misunderstanding) and thinking about a problem.

Division also lends itself to the creation of alternate algorithms. Traditionally, students are taught to divide, multiply, subtract, compare, and bring down when doing long division, and they may have even created a mnemonic device for helping them to remember those steps. Some students, though, will find ways to divide larger numbers without having to follow the traditional procedure, as seen in Figure 4–7. This student used the grab method, where he took out multiples of the divisor from the dividend and then on the side indicated how many groups (or "grabs") of the divisor he took out. That is, he first subtracted four hundred, which is one hundred groups of four (the divisor). He continued to take out multiples of the divisor until he couldn't take any more

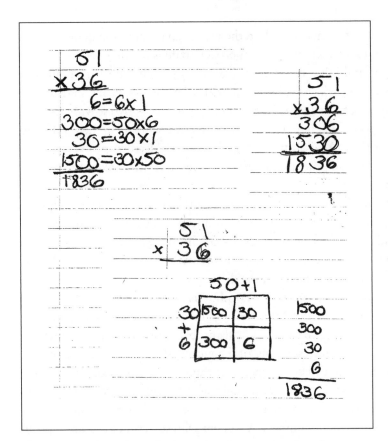

Figure 4–6 *A student shows several ways to solve the same problem.*

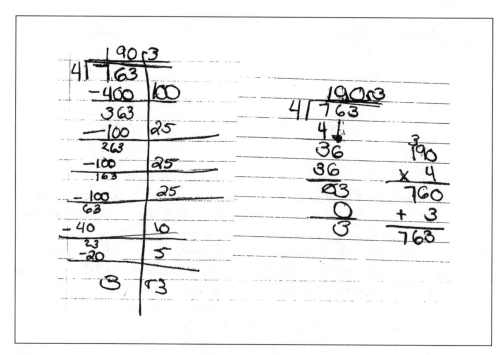

Figure 4–7 *Two ways to solve a division problem*

out, leaving a remainder. He then added up the grabs, giving him the quotient with remainder. As students experiment with this approach to division, they soon learn that it doesn't matter what multiples they use first; eventually, if they keep grabbing out multiples of the divisor, they will get the same quotient. That is to say, one student may keep grabbing out forty because that is an easy number for her to work with. Eventually, she will subtract forty out enough times, and then she will add up her grabs and arrive at the same quotient. Again, this strategy for solving division problems is one that is developed *first* through the use of manipulatives and then linked to the symbolic representation.

Some students make the connection that because they can use repeated addition with multiplication, they can use the inverse of addition, subtraction, with division. For example, if a student is asked to solve 1,834 ÷ 35, he may subtract thirty-five over and over again from the dividend until he cannot subtract it out anymore, and then he will count how many times he subtracted the divisor.

The wonderful thing about alternative algorithms is that they develop out of a student's growing understanding of a concept, without having conventions and rules applied to them. These invented approaches to solving problems provide us, their teachers, with great insight into their understanding of a concept, their confidence as mathematicians, and their development as independent thinkers. It is so exciting to see a student solve a problem in a way we never thought of! We need to encourage our students to solve mathematical problems in a way that makes sense to them, so that they are thinking and reasoning about numbers. A student who solves multiplication problems only through repeated addition and counting, or by drawing a picture, may need to be exposed to and guided toward more efficient strategies. That is not to say that we should dismiss their approach to solving a problem, but rather, through exposing them to and discussing the way other students solve problems, we can coach them to the next level.

CLASSROOM-TESTED TIP

Let problem solving be a primary element in your mathematics instruction. Present the children with a rich math story to solve and observe what strategies they use to solve it. While the students are working, make a note of the students who use efficient and understandable strategies to solve the problem and have them share out to the whole class at the end of the math lesson. Ask a student to explain in his own words how his classmate solved a problem.

Using Equations to Solve Problems and Visualize Ideas

As mentioned before, we do a great disservice to our students when we teach procedures and algorithms without letting them develop their own understanding of a concept. However, we would be negligent as well if we did not help students make the connection between ideas and equations and see how equations can help us solve problems and visualize ideas.

An equation represents a whole idea. For example, $\frac{1}{4} + \frac{1}{2} = \frac{3}{4}$. In order for this equation to have meaning for students, other than as a memorized fact, they must understand several things. First, they have to understand what $\frac{1}{4}$, $\frac{1}{2}$, and $\frac{3}{4}$ mean (they represent different-size parts of a whole), and, perhaps more importantly, they must understand what the equals sign represents. The notion that the equals sign balances an equation is essential. Here is one experience a teacher had when assessing her students' understanding of this concept:

TEACHER: I am going to write an equation on the board and I want you give me your thoughts. (*She writes 15 = 8 + 7.*)

STUDENT: You can't write it like that.

TEACHER: No? Why not?

STUDENT: Because the answer has to come last, and fifteen is the answer.

TEACHER: OK. What does this symbol mean (*pointing to the equals sign*)?

STUDENT: It means the answer. Like, if I had the problem three times six equals eighteen, the equals sign tells you that the answer is next, which is eighteen.

TEACHER: Does anyone else have any thoughts?

STUDENT: I think the answer can come first, because eight plus seven equals fifteen, so what you're really saying is fifteen equals fifteen.

TEACHER: It sounds like Aidan has noticed something about what's on each side of the equals sign. Let's look at this equation. (*She writes 3 × 4 = 4 × 3 on the board.*)

STUDENT: Well, three times four equals twelve, and four times three equals twelve, so both sides equal the same thing.

TEACHER: Let's try one more. (*She writes 15 ÷ 3 = 10 – 5.*) Is this true?

STUDENT: Yes, it's true because fifteen divided by three equals five, and ten minus five equals five, so both sides of the equals sign equal five.

TEACHER: What, then, does the equals sign mean?

STUDENT: It means that whatever is on one side of the equals sign must be worth the same as what's on the other side of it.

TEACHER: Exactly. The equals sign balances what's on each side. They must be equal in value, even if they don't look the same. That's why you can write fifteen equals eight plus seven, because each side of the equation is equal in value. In your math journal, write an equation and explain what the equals sign means in that equation.

This conversation highlights a misconception that must be cleared up before equations have real meaning for students. Certainly, without this fundamental understanding of what the equals sign represents, students will struggle with algebraic concepts and higher math. By simply assessing students' understanding of this concept through informal conversation and then asking them to process what they've learned through journal writing, we can help to ensure that they master this very basic concept.

Once we are comfortable that our students understand what an equation is, including what its parts represent, and that they have constructed their own knowledge and understanding about a concept, then we can begin to introduce symbols and equations associated with certain concepts. For example, in the primary grades, we talk about putting groups together and counting the total. We do this over and over with manipulatives before we introduce the symbols + and =. However, once students fully understand that when we put groups together, we are adding, then they can rely on using those symbols to create equations associated with that action.

By fifth grade, most students have been exposed to some algebraic concepts, such as solving for an unknown *n*, for example, $n = 25 \times 4$, or $100 - n = 40$. These equations have no meaning to students if they have not yet mastered the concept of what the equals sign means, as mentioned previously, or what each of the other symbols (×, –, etc.) signify. Once students have a deep understanding of these basic symbols, they have the power to create their own equations to interpret the world around them. For example, consider this problem:

A plant grows 5 centimeters a day. How tall will it be on the third day? On the eighth day? Write an equation that shows how tall the plant will be on a given day if *n* is the number of the day.

Students may choose to create a table, such as the one in Figure 4–8, showing the height of the plant each day so that they can clearly see that on day one, the plant is five centimeters, on day two it is ten centimeters, on day three it is fifteen centimeters, and so on. Then, they can create the equation $n \times 5 =$ height of plant in centimeters. A pattern has been discovered and an equation has been created to explain the pattern. That is powerful mathematical thinking!

Day	Height in Centimeters
1	5
2	10
3	15
4	20

Figure 4–8 *Chart showing plant's growth*

Numbers and symbols also serve to reduce the cognitive demands on the learner. For example, when working to solve a complex problem, students can use numbers and symbols to record intermediary steps without having to remember them. They can then refer back to the notes they made when they need them.

The Role of the Teacher

In the area of numbers and symbols, the teacher acts as a coach, paying careful attention to the moment when a student is ready to move from concrete representations to more abstract ones. For us to be able to do this, we must provide our students with many opportunities to show what they understand about a topic, through manipulatives, paper representations, and verbal explanations. They also must be exposed to different ways of solving problems so that they can compare their strategies with others and refine theirs to an efficient, meaningful strategy upon which they can draw in the future. Equations help to form complete pictures and explain actions through symbols. For example, the equation $824 \div 22 = $ _____ means 824 divided into 22 equal groups or into groups of 22. Allowing students to use the shortcut of symbols and equations must not be the result of shortcutting them through the process of developing their own understanding of mathematical concepts and ideas. The time we spend in concept development, assessment, and determining the right moment at which to introduce numbers and symbols is time well invested and will help to develop competent, confident young mathematicians.

One of the most important roles of the mathematics teacher is requiring students to justify their thinking. It is not enough for students simply to give an answer. We must challenge them to defend the strategy they choose to solve a problem and to prove that they are right. Questions we might ask to do this include:

- How did you solve this problem?

- Why did you choose that strategy?

- Why do you think you're right?

- How else could you have solved it?

By pushing our students to think beyond just getting the right answer, we are helping them to think more deeply about the mathematics they are learning.

Helping students gain flexibility and fluency in mathematical thinking should be one of the goals of any math program. There are many ways in which we can help our students to develop these skills. Try these activities out as warm-ups, sponges (time fillers), or homework activities.

- *Renaming a Number:* Help students to think about different ways we can name numbers. For example: $112 = 100 + 10 + 12$ or $50 + 50 + 10 + 2$. A wonderful game for helping students develop fluency with computation and flexibility with numbers is the commercially available 24 Game. It is a mental game that requires students to combine four numbers in such a way that they end up with a total of twenty-four.

- *Target Number:* This activity is similar to renaming a number. You select a target number and students must think of as many possible ways to reach the target number as they can. For example, 12 can be reached by dividing 144 by 12 or by doubling 6.

- *Who Am I?* Students are given clues about numbers and must guess the number. For example, "I am an odd number that is a multiple of three and I am between sixteen and twenty-five" (twenty-one). Students can generate their own "Who Am I?" riddles.

- *Buzz:* Students gather in a circle. A number is selected, such as six, and as the students count off starting at one, those students who would say a multiple of six instead say, "Buzz."

- *Predict Then Count:* The group gathers in a circle and counts off by ones. The leader then selects a value to count by (such as one-half) and before counting, students can predict what they think will be the last number announced. For example, if there are nineteen children in the class and they are counting by one-half each time, students might predict that ten will be the last number announced, or some may correctly predict that nine and one-half will be the last number. While the children are counting, record the numbers they announce on chart paper. After counting, discuss how the predictions compared with the actual number and solicit strategies for how students figured it out, and look for patterns in the chart.

- *What's the Question?* Give students an answer, such as "The answer is fifty. What's the question?" Student responses might be "How much is two quarters [or half of a dollar]?" or "How many pounds does my seven-year-old brother weigh?" and so on.

- *Starting Where?* Ask students to count by five, for example, and they respond by asking you, "Starting where?" Choose different numbers to start with, such as "Count by fives starting at nineteen." Get them to count over landmark numbers, such as one hundred, to build their fluency with larger numbers as well.

Questions for Discussion

1. How can we help students make the connection between concrete representations and symbolic ones?

2. What is the value of alternative or invented algorithms?

3. How can we ensure our students have a deep understanding of a concept before moving them to symbolic representations?

4. What is the value in asking students to justify their thinking?

5. What is the role of the teacher in introducing numbers and symbols to students?

CHAPTER 5

Using Tables and Graphs to Record, Organize, and Communicate Ideas

It's Not Just About Bar Graphs Anymore!

How many times do we ask students to create a graph of their choice to represent some type of data, only to get page after page of bar graphs? Have you ever looked at data displays in science or social studies and seen stem-and-leaf plots or boxes and whiskers? Not likely! Bar graphs seem to be the data display most teachers use and most students feel comfortable using, regardless of whether the graph is an appropriate form for representing the data. For primary students, bar graphs and tally charts are familiar territory. But just as with numbers, data and data displays increase in complexity as students progress in their mathematical knowledge. Students need to understand that what they are graphing helps determine how they will graph the information, and that some displays are just not appropriate for certain data types. In this chapter, we take a look at some ways to incorporate a variety of graphing displays and then look at the analysis that needs to take place once the graphing is complete.

Why Graph?

Are we asking students to graph for the sake of graphing, or are we asking them to graph in order to answer a legitimate question? The purpose of graphing is to organize data in a meaningful display in order to make analysis of the data easier. The purpose of collecting data is to answer a question or questions. According to NCTM, students at this grade level need to "formulate questions that can be addressed with data and collect, organize, and display relevant data to answer them" (NCTM 2002, 177). Data isn't a set of disconnected numbers used solely to practice finding mean, median, and mode. Data is information: information gathered in an attempt to see a trend, solve a problem, or support a hypothesis. Students in grades 3 through 5 have a lot of interests that can be tapped for the purposes of learning about statistical displays, but far too often they are limited to working with a meaningless set of numbers. When this happens, no knowledge can be gained concerning the appropriate selection of the statistical display, and no knowledge is gained concerning the information the graph reveals beyond the arbitrary numbers used. Imagine the excitement that can be generated when students begin to see statistical representations about themselves or about topics of interest to them. When students have a stake in the data and an interest in the question being investigated, their analysis of the data becomes so much more than a series of numbers generated to find measures of central tendency. The standards-based classroom may at times seem limited in the type of graphing display that is promoted at a given grade level. Students in grades 3 through 5 will move from simple bar graphs, tally charts, and pictographs to double-bar graphs, double-line graphs, line plots, stem-and-leaf plots, histograms, and possibly boxes and whiskers. There are two important things to keep in mind: once a graph has been taught, it should continue to be used and continue to be a choice when students are determining the most appropriate display to represent their data, and as always, students need to begin with the concrete and move toward the symbolic representation of the data.

From Real Graphs to Pictographs

Ask any primary teacher about his graphing activities and he will begin with a description of the real graphs he creates in his classroom. A real graph uses actual objects in the representation. For example, the teacher might ask a question concerning the types of shoes students are wearing. The comparison might be made between those students wearing shoes that tie versus those that don't or between the color of shoes. Students would then create a graph using their shoes, and then with one shoe on and one shoe off, students would discuss the display in front of them. By the time students hit third grade, you may have a hard time convincing them to take off their shoes to create a graph, and even if you do convince them, you need to be prepared for the choruses of "phew" as shoes are removed. It's going to happen! An alternative to real graphs, but a natural progression, is the pictograph, and like the real graph, the pictograph does not need to be on a numeric scale. Generally pictographs with a scale can be used to help students practice skip counting as they use the scale to represent the quantities being graphed. Using pictures or representations of the objects in the graph instead of the real thing provides a little more flexibility in what we can graph. Take time, however, to help students connect the two types of graphs. It may not be obvious to all students that the two data displays are related. In order for the data to be meaningful and easier to graph, limit the comparisons you ask the students to make within the data to three to five categories. If the number of categories is much larger, it will be more difficult to answer the question that the graph is supposed to address.

Data can come from a variety of sources. Students love taking and giving surveys. This provides a wealth of graphable information. For example, one favorite topic to address with pictographs is the type of pets students have or would like to have. Adding the "would like to have" category allows those students without pets an opportunity to participate. Another option would be to have a category of no pets. Students could bring in pictures of their pets, draw pictures of their pets, or cut pictures out of a magazine of a favorite type of pet. Trying to graph all of the different types of pets could create too many categories, and some categories might have only one or two pets. Instead, why not create specific categories that allow your students to put different animals in like categories, such as pets with fur, pets without fur, pets with two legs, pets with four legs, pets that walk, pets that fly, or pets that slither? Students can imagine seeing their pets on the graphs as they put pictures on the graph. Another option would be to take advantage of the die cuts that most schools have available and use the shapes to represent the animals or objects to be graphed. Most craft stores now stock tubs of foam shapes that come in all sizes and themes. These shapes make wonderful graphs and they can be reused over and over again for a variety of graphing activities.

At this level, the data used in pictographs should be sufficient enough to allow for a scale to be used in representing the information, and remember: always start with a question that gives students a reason for collecting the data in the first place. Consider the following scenario:

> **The cafeteria manager wants to make sure students have an opportunity to buy their favorite foods at lunch so she asked Mrs. Gebhart's class to create a survey to find out what food students like best. The survey was given to all of the 225 students in the 5th grade and asked students to identify their favorite foods from the following list: pizza, hot dogs, chicken nuggets, or cheeseburgers.**

Narrowing the choices to four possibilities in a survey of 225 students would provide students with enough meaningful data so that they could reach a conclusion about the favorite food of students

CLASSROOM-TESTED TIP

Creating and administering a survey with a large data base (such as 225 students) would take more time than most teachers want to spend on any one activity, but there are other ways to collect data. For instance, in the cafeteria situation, why not use a number cube, assigning each food to a number? Blank cubes (see Figure 5–1) can also be used, and stickers can be affixed to the sides of the cubes. Students can then write the names of the categories on the stickers and roll the die to collect their data. Working in groups of 3 to 4 students the number of total rolls recorded by the entire class should equal, in this case 225. Spinners can also be used for this purpose. Clear overhead spinners can be placed on top of pre-drawn templates with categories written in each of the spaces.

Other topics with possible graphing situations include

What is your favorite color?
What type of music do you like best?
What is your favorite sport to play?
What is your favorite sport to watch?
What is your favorite flavor of ice cream?
What is your favorite food?
What kind of pets do you have?

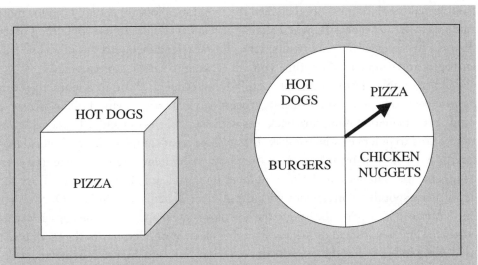

Figure 5–1 *Cubes or spinners can be used to collect data.*

No matter what the topic, remember to begin with a question, and once the data is collected and displayed, use the display to answer the question.

Line Plots or Line Graphs

In order for students to understand when to use appropriate data displays, they have to be given multiple opportunities to see how the graphs differ in purpose. A student who uses a line graph to graph a class' preferences for food in a cafeteria obviously doesn't understand the real use of a line graph. Likewise, a student who uses a bar graph to show hourly temperature changes hasn't quite grasped the intent of a bar graph.

A line plot allows students an opportunity to count objects on a numeric scale. Generally speaking, an X is placed above the numeric value to represent each piece of data. Because the line plot can be compared with a bar graph, students have little trouble making the connection between the two. Line plots are actually fun for most students to create, especially when a creative teacher decides to use something other than *X*'s to represent the data points. Line plots also lend themselves to other curricular topics and can be used anytime you are looking to see each piece of data.

One example of how a line plot can add an element of fun to a math class can be found on the candy shelf of any grocery store. During many holiday seasons, candy makers market miniature packages with small pieces of candy. These packages can be used to practice estimation skills as well as create graphs with real-world materials. Each student begins by estimating how many items are in her bag and then counts the items in her bag. Using a number line, students place their bag above the appropriate spot that corresponds with the number of items in their bag. Once everyone has placed his bag on the graph, the line plot takes shape. Using the bags as markers on the line plot instead of *X*'s adds another element of relevancy to the math being used. Keep in mind that the purpose of collecting data is to answer a question, so instead of just graphing for the sake of graphing, the teacher needs to create a legitimate question. The question could center on the weight of the bags and the number of candies inside or the price relationship to the regular-size candy bags. Whatever the question, make sure that the data collected is appropriate and provides information that will allow students the opportunity to make an informed conclusion. Students can represent the data on paper as well, substituting *X*'s for the bags as they create their own graphs. Most students will be able to see the similarities of a bar graph and a line plot. Measures of central tendency are fairly easy to determine with a line plot. One advantage to using a line plot is that when you are done, the data is already in order and students will have no problem recognizing the mode and finding the median. As an extension to this activity, ask the class to apply the information gained concerning the smaller packages to estimate how many candies would be in the larger packages. Marilyn Burns has a wonderful description of a line plot activity in her book *A Collection of Math Lessons, from Grades 3 Through 6* (1987). In the activity, students create line plots with small boxes of raisins (a much healthier way of collecting data). Here again the teacher can have the students put a piece of tape on the back of their boxes and use them to graph the points on the line plot instead of using *X*'s.

Continuous line graphs are different from line plots, but many times students fail to see that difference. While a line plot counts data along a numeric scale, a continuous line graph shows pieces of data along a scale, but takes it one step further and connects the pieces of data to show additional data in between the points. The connecting lines oftentimes cause confusion among students if they don't realize that the lines, too, are pieces of data. An easy way to help students understand this would be to graph temperature changes, growth of a plant, or changes in the length of a shadow. By recording the data on temperature, students should be able to see that the temperature or height gradually changes throughout the time span being recorded and doesn't just suddenly jump to the next piece of graphed data. Once students see the connection between the pieces of data, they should begin to see that certain types of data cannot be graphed using continuous line graphs. For example, you can't graph the number of students in your class who have computers using a continuous line plot, but students could go to a website for information on how the average number of computers owned by a family has changed over the past twenty years and graph that information. You can't graph the amount of money items cost in a grocery store on a line graph, but you can research prices of some common items and graph the price changes that have occurred over time. There are some great websites for helping students collect data for graphing change over time.

- The United States Census Bureau website has great data from the 2000 census. (www.census.gov)

- The Central Intelligence Agency has a *World Factbook* that contains data on a number of topics, including how many telephones a country has. (www.cia.gov/cia/publications/factbook/index.html)

- The United States Department of Agriculture site lists information on all fifty states relevant to population, farming, and exports, among other topics. (www.ers.usda.gov/statefacts)

- Information on weather statistics can be found on the National Oceanic and Atmospheric Administration website from the National Climatic Data Center. (www.ncdc.noaa.gov/oa/ncdc.html)

- Data on the solar system can be found at www.nineplanets.org/data.html.

Try Working Backward

Another way to help students understand continuous line graphs would be to work backward and start with the graph. Then ask students to make up the situation that might have been used to create the graph in the first place.

Students in Mrs. Hamilton's fourth-grade class were given the graph in Figure 5–2 and asked to create a story about what data might have been collected to create this graph.

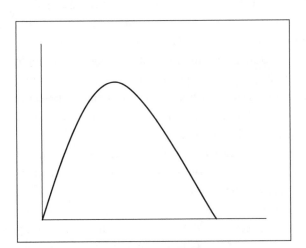

Figure 5–2 *Working backward with a line graph*

Patty's group wrote that they thought the graph represented a roller-coaster ride. The height of the coaster was being measured as it climbed up and then dropped down. Daryl's group took another approach to the situation; they concluded that the graph was of a skateboarder, and the height of his jump was being measured as he jumped over a ramp.

Trish's group wrote that they knew it must be measuring the loudness of the noise in the cafeteria at lunchtime. It is quiet when students come into the cafeteria but the noise levels grow throughout the lunch period, until finally all noise has to stop as students prepare to go back to their classes.

Each group expressed their ideas in broad terms but each identified a correct situation in which a line graph might be used. This type of activity allows students to look closely at the graph and analyze the peaks and valleys for the type of information that might have been used to create the graph. This activity could also be extended by having students create their own blank graphs for others to analyze or challenging students to draw a graph that might represent a certain situation.

As students collect data for representation on any line graph, they also need to be aware of the scale that should be used and the appropriate use of each axis. It does make a difference! When students are graphing change over a period of time, the horizontal (x) axis needs to be labeled for time and the vertical (y) axis needs to be scaled for the measured data, whatever that may be. The graphs are read left to right so that the change over the period of time can be seen. Line graphs also provide wonderful opportunities to make predictions based on the shape of the line as the two points of data are graphed. The trends or the direction the line seems to be taking on a line graph can provide opportunities for additional conversations about predictions on what will happen in five or ten years.

Stem-and-Leaf Plots

In addition to line plots and line graphs, stem-and-leaf plots are also ways to show all of the data points. The difference here is in the way the points are represented on the stem and leaf. Instead of a typical graphlike display, the stem and leaf represents the values of each data point using the numbers themselves. For example, to start a stem and leaf, a student would first need to determine the stem. It might be a single digit or it might be larger. If the data to be graphed ranged from twelve to ninety-nine, then the stems would all be single digits starting with at least one (which represents the tens place in the number twelve). The leaves would then represent the ones place and need to be opposite the ten values. (See Figure 5–3.)

The same can be done for larger numbers; the stem would just increase in the number of digits to allow for the larger values. In later grades students will work with back-to-back stem-and-leaf plots to allow for comparisons of two sets of data.

Because all of the data points are represented on the stem-and-leaf graph, the shape of the data becomes an important piece of the data conversation. Students may even comment that the leaves on the graph could be made to look like bars if they were shaded in and rotated around. Students should be encouraged to look at the data and think about the following questions: How much of the data is in the middle? Are their

Data: 12, 33, 23, 64, 58, 37, 99, 33, 61, 84, 89, 55, 75, 19, 20	
1	2, 9
2	0, 3
3	3, 3, 7
4	
5	5, 8
6	1, 4
7	5
8	4, 9
9	9

KEY: $\boxed{7}\boxed{5}$ = 75

In this example, students did not need to start the stem with zero since no number was less than twelve, although it would have been perfectly fine if they had. They also had no leaf for four since no piece of data was in the forties. While some texts will differ on this, keeping the four as a stem even without a data point is important. Notice that the data in each of the leaves is in order from least to greatest as it moves away from the stem. It is easy to identify the mode, and finding the median would be just as easy since the data is already ordered.

Figure 5–3 *Stem-and-leaf plot*

any outliers that would skew the overall measures of the data? Does the data seem to be equally spaced out or are there gaps in the numbers? Having these conversations about the shape of the data instead of only looking at mean, median, and mode as descriptors of the data helps students have a better understanding of the data as a whole.

Other topics that lend themselves to stem-and-leaf plots are

- ages of presidents at the time they took office or their ages at their death

- quiz or test scores

- number of books read by students during the summer

Students with an understanding of stem-and-leaf plots should easily be able to make the connection to histograms since both are frequency tables. Although student work with histograms at this level will be more toward interpretation than creation, the connections and similarities can still be made.

C L A S S R O O M - T E S T E D   T I P

In order to create a profile of students at the beginning of the year, many teachers take an interest survey to see what sports, TV shows, music, subjects, or foods they like best. Use these surveys to tap into student interests as graphing discussions occur.

Histograms

Creating histograms is not generally taught in grades 3 through 5. However, many textbooks and newspapers do use histograms to display data. For this reason, it might be prudent to use some time to at least make a quick comparison of histograms, bar graphs, and line plots so that students have a little background for understanding data when they see histograms in other texts.

Circle Graphs

Helping students understand and interpret circle graphs (pie graphs) in grades 3 through 5 may be much easier than having them represent those same graphs. While there are a number of commercially produced graphing programs available that make the job a lot easier, producing circle graphs can be a little tricky for students at this stage. There is, however, a good rationale for using circle graphs with students in these grades. The use of circle graphs helps students visualize the relationships of the sizes of the subgroups independently or combined with each other and with the whole. Identifying the whole is much easier to do with a circle graph since the circle it-self represents the whole. Another key aspect of the circle graph is that while it looks much different than the bar graph, the two can be used in representing the same type of data. In fact, since students are so familiar with bar graphs, using them to help students understand circle graphs just makes sense.

From Bars to Circles

The following question was presented to fourth-grade students in Mrs. Johnson's math class:

> **Of the following snack foods, what is your all-time favorite: popcorn, french fries, potato chips, or pretzels?**

Students were allowed to vote for only one of these foods, and then using the collected data, they created a class bar graph. Figure 5–4 shows how their sample graph looked.

Mrs. Johnson created the class graph using strips of construction paper on a graph-lined easel pad and then cut out the bars of the graph. She glued the bars end to end to form a strip. The strips of construction paper glued end to end looked like the illustration in Figure 5–5.

Then Mrs. Johnson glued the two ends of the strips together, forming a circle. The students now saw the relationship between the bar graph and circle graph and how the two could be used to represent the same data. Granted, all of this was modeled by Mrs. Johnson, but when one of her students asked, "What happens if more people vote? How will you put the rest of the people in the circle graph?" rather than answer the question, Mrs. Johnson asked them first to write down what they thought

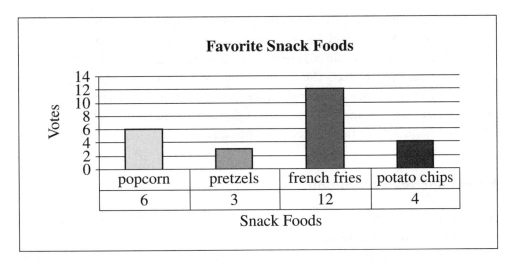

Figure 5-4 *Snack food graph*

would happen and then she allowed them to explore the situation in small groups. She gave each group the same scenario:

When given the choice of the following things to do, how many students voted for each?
1. **Watching a movie**
2. **Playing a video game**
3. **Going to an amusement park**
4. **Playing a board game**

She told each group how many students they could survey, but instead of surveying actual students, each group used a four-section spinner with one of the possible answers written in each of the four sections. The number of spins each group made was determined by the number of students Mrs. Johnson told each group they could survey, and the number was different for each group. Once the groups finished their simulated surveys, they graphed the results using a bar graph. The scale was the same for each graph. With their bar graphs complete, each group proceeded to cut out the individual bars and glue them end to end as Mrs. Johnson had done earlier and then placed the completed circles in the center of the room for all to see. Before any discussion took place, Mrs. Johnson again ask them write down whether they were right about their original assumption and then what they thought about the results. The class

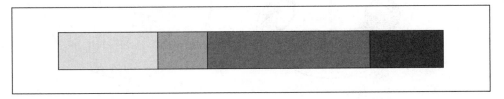

Figure 5-5 *Mrs. Johnson glued the bars of the graph end to end to form a strip.*

discussion focused on the predictions the students had made before the exploration and the results each group had. Some groups had correctly predicted that while the circle would get bigger, you could still connect the ends of the bars, while others were surprised to see the ends connect. The students now had a clearer understanding of what happens in a circle graph as the sample space increases. Instead of just telling them the answer when the first question arose, Mrs. Johnson allowed them to construct some of their own meaning as they represented the data.

From Concrete to Symbolic

As with other concepts, moving students through the stages of concrete to pictorial to symbolic is crucial in helping students understand circle graphs. Once students have a clear understanding of what the sections in the circle graph represent, teachers can move forward in having students create circle graphs on their own. One method has students starting with a paper circle and folding that circle into equal parts. Halves, fourths, and eighths work well for this. Each folded section of the circle now represents a piece of the whole in which students can place concrete objects. For third-grade students just starting out with basic problems involving circle graphs, this visual representation of a circle graph provides them not only with a clear picture of the graph's purpose but also with a glimpse into how the graph is created. At this very basic level, students can begin to see how the sections of graph relate to the whole circle, and by removing the concrete objects from the sections and shading them in, students should be able to begin to see the connections between the shaded areas and the areas with the concrete representations. (See Figure 5–6.)

By the time students reach grade 5, and fractions and percents become a part of their instruction, circle graphs can be extended so that they are more symbolic in nature.

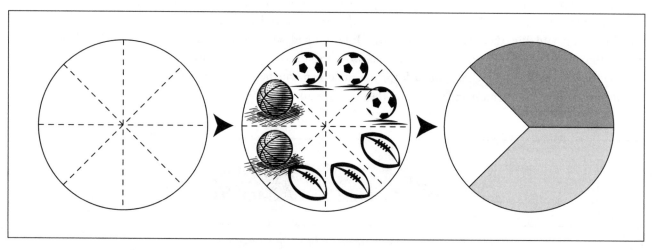

Figure 5–6 *Moving from concrete to symbolic*

The Role of the Teacher

In the area of graphic representations, one of the most important roles a teacher can play is in getting students to see the differences in purpose of certain graphs and how crucial it is to choose the correct representation for the information at hand. Yes, we all know the importance of placing a title on a graph and labeling the *x*- and *y*-axes because that gives important information to the reader, but is it more important than using the appropriate type of graph? Teachers also need to ensure that their students have opportunities to look at data collection and representation of that data as part of a question to be answered. A list of arbitrary numbers to graph does not help students in seeing the importance of graphical display and data analysis. So-called naked math serves no purpose in helping students internalize these concepts. Graphing needs to be in context with choices. In the area of data analysis, students can take a lot more meaning away from mean, median, and mode when context is used, but those are not the only analyses of the data and graph that need to take place. In addition to the measures of central tendency, teachers should help students analyze the graph in other ways. By asking questions about the shape of the graphed data or how far apart the data points are, teachers can help students begin to see information about the population being graphed even before they do the computations on the data.

Graphing data is an excellent tool for cross-curricular and multicultural activities. Because textbooks, newspapers, and the Internet are all available as data sources, teachers should make a conscious effort to include multiple opportunities for students to tap into these resources.

Figure 5–7 *Circle graphs provide a way for students to represent information.*

Questions for Discussion

1. How can allowing student choice in graphic display provide information on students' understanding of the purpose of each graph?

2. Why is it important to look at data collection as a means for answering a question?

3. How can teachers help students in connecting the uses and purposes of the various graphic displays?

4. What are some of the steps that can be used as students are led through the concrete to the symbolic stages of graphing?

5. What are some of the reasons students need context in graphing?

CHAPTER 6

Assessing Students' Representations

Assessment is the process of gathering evidence about a student's knowledge of, ability to use, and disposition toward, mathematics and of making inferences from that evidence for a variety of purposes.

—National Council of Teachers of Mathematics,
Assessment Standards for School Mathematics

The ability to represent math ideas in multiple ways is extremely useful as students grow in their mathematical knowledge. By being able to draw on words, pictures, numbers, tables, and so on, students are empowered to understand and represent the world around them and their internal thought processes. However, these models that serve as a student's tool box must be constructed because they are not taught or given by the teacher. Rather, they emerge from a student's actions in a given situation. When faced with the issue of assessing our students' representations, we must ask ourselves two questions: Why are we assessing the representations our students make, and how are we going to use the information gained from the assessment tool? In this chapter, we discuss the value in assessing those representations, and we look at different ways in which we can assess our students.

Why Assess?

Teachers assess every day, either formally or informally, and for different reasons. The most common assessment we do is that which helps us to make decisions about our instruction. We make daily adjustments to our plans based on our students' needs. Do some students need additional time to explore a topic? Are some students ready to move forward with the application of the concept? Have a group of students demonstrated mastery and need to be challenged? Are the majority of students confused about a topic and need a new approach? Assessment is essential in helping us make these decisions.

Another reason we assess is to give parents and students feedback. Most students want to know where they excel and in what areas they need to improve. Parents are especially interested in how their child is performing in relationship to other students as well as the grade-level content. Assessment (especially performance assessment) can help us give them this information. By seeing how their child does when faced with a task with specific objectives, parents can get a clear idea of their child's performance at any given moment. Finally, we may use assessment to help us assign a grade to a student's performance. Evaluating student learning is a complex task that is supported by quality assessment, which can be used to justify a teacher's decision to assign a certain grade to a student.

Assessing Representation

In grades 3 through 5, the main goal of the representation process standard is simply to be able to represent the mathematics and represent student understanding of the mathematics. Many students will become competent at representing and will look for more accurate and efficient ways to do so, while some students will still struggle with what it means to make a representation of their thinking. We all strive to help our students become proficient in mathematics and all teachers want to be able to judge fairly the work put forth by our students. How, then, do we assess a student's ability to represent her thinking? In this book we have been looking at how students can represent their thinking in a number of ways. Words, pictures, diagrams, symbols, and numbers are all elements of what we have been calling multiple representations. But when we assess a student's representations, are we looking for the correctness of her answer? Are we looking for an appropriate algorithm that can be used to solve a problem? Are we looking to see what steps the student went through as she reached a solution? Are we assessing only what she could put down on paper? Are we assessing the conceptual understandings or the procedural ones? And finally, what tools do we use in assessing student representations?

Math classrooms today bear little resemblance to classrooms ten to fifteen years ago. Gone are the days when students were asked to solve problems without justifying their thinking. Students today are being required to demonstrate their thinking and reasoning through explanations and justifications of their work. We are being challenged to find and use assessments that are rich and have the range of uses that will allow our students an opportunity to demonstrate their levels of understanding. If a task is not rich, if it is not cognitively demanding, then students will not be able to adequately demonstrate their knowledge. What information will we gain from a task that has only a right or wrong answer? Today, more than ever, information about students' levels of understanding and mastery is all too important as we look for ways to adjust our instruction to meet the needs of not only our curriculum but more importantly our students.

We have a number of valuable options available to us when assessing our students' representations. We might

- observe students and engage them in conversations about their work

- interview and conference with students

- use a performance-based task

- collect samples of their work (e.g., portfolios)

The questions are What should we assess and When should we assess? Choosing the correct assessment is determined by our purpose in assessing, as described earlier. In this chapter we look at different forms of assessment and determine how we might use them when looking at our students' representations.

Observations

During a math lesson, it is not uncommon for us to walk around and see what our students are doing. Are they on task? Do they appear excited, frustrated, or confused about the activity? Are they working purposefully or merely attempting to appear busy?

Ongoing observations allow teachers opportunities to see their students in a variety of situations during the math class, and while most of those observations are informal in nature, they should be a part of the regular classroom routine. The important thing to remember is the documentation that needs to take place during that observation time or shortly thereafter. Without some form of documentation, those mental notes we make as we walk around the room become lost and may fail to provide any lasting information.

One way to make the classroom observation meaningful is to structure a task in which all students are engaged in the same topic at the same time. During the planning of that task, the teacher needs to create a few focused questions to ask during this time and determine how the information will be documented.

Fourth-grade teacher Mrs. Turner engages in what she likes to call "clipboard cruising." As students are working on an activity, whether cooperatively or independently, she walks around the room with her clipboard, a set of sticky notes, and focus questions. Stopping by Karen's desk, she asks, "How does your representation of the first part of this problem match the question?" If Karen is able to connect her notations to the problem in a meaningful way or if she has created a picture that shows an appropriate level of mastery, Mrs. Turner notes that on Karen's card or sticky note. She may ask one question or a series of questions, but she is always trying to get the students to explain their thinking as they work through the task. Other questions she might ask include "How is your representation of this solution similar (or different) from one you did yesterday?" "Can you explain the picture you drew for this part of the problem?" and "Why did you choose to organize your work in this way?" As students respond to her questions, she quickly jots down some of their responses on their sticky note. If a student can justify his representation of the problem, if he can provide evidence that he has used his representations to make the problem more meaningful or to find a solution, she makes quick notes of his efforts. She can also clearly see when a student is unable to adequately justify her response or when her representations seem to be taking her in another direction, indicating to the teacher that she needs to find a way to redirect the student's thinking. Once class is over, she either adds to her notes if time allows or files them in student or class folders for later. Mrs. Turner is looking for a number of things as she cruises the room: is student work organized, have the children been able to communicate their thinking, have they chosen to use one of the problem-solving strategies appropriate for this problem? The observation is purposeful, it is organized, and because Mrs. Turner records the information, it provides lasting evidence of student work. She won't get to all students every day, but it has become a part of her classroom routine and students know what to expect and aren't surprised or caught off guard when she stops by their desk.

Interviews and Conferences

In addition to observing students as they work, having a structured time to meet with students one-on-one and confer with them concerning their progress provides valuable information. Planned conferences allow for a much more structured venue for engaging students in math conversations. While finding the time to actually have these conversations or interviews with students may be difficult, elementary teachers are wonderfully creative in utilizing stolen moments of time, especially when their efforts yield lasting results.

In Mr. Cody's fifth-grade class, he has regularly scheduled interview times with students during recess periods and before or after school when he can focus his attention on a particular student. He starts early in the year talking with his students about the interview process and has an introductory meeting lasting only five to ten minutes when he asks them about their attitudes concerning math. He also likes to see what areas they feel are strengths and/or weaknesses. Keeping the interview short and nonthreatening is essential to getting students to feel comfortable and willing to talk about their perceived abilities. He tries to make sure he asks each student the same or at least similar questions so that he has like information on each student. As the year progresses, he continues with both formal and informal interviews with his students. Sometimes his inquiries are about a particular task, and he may ask them questions such as, "Why did you choose this representation?" and "Was there another way to solve that problem?" He wants his students to look at alternate methods of solving problems and representing the solutions, so he encourages them to always look back and rethink the problems instead of being satisfied with one method.

In an interview with Jordon on his work with the task Chairs and Stools, Mr. Cody was particularly interested in how Jordon handled the first part of challenge portion of the task. He wasn't able to see Jordon's thinking, so he asked him how he determined his answer without additional computation. (See Figure 6–1.)

Jordon explained that since the challenge problem asked him what would happen if five of the legs were broken, he knew that if four legs were broken that was one chair and the fifth leg meant that a chair now became a stool, so he subtracted two chairs and added one stool. It was clear that Jordon had internalized the process, but

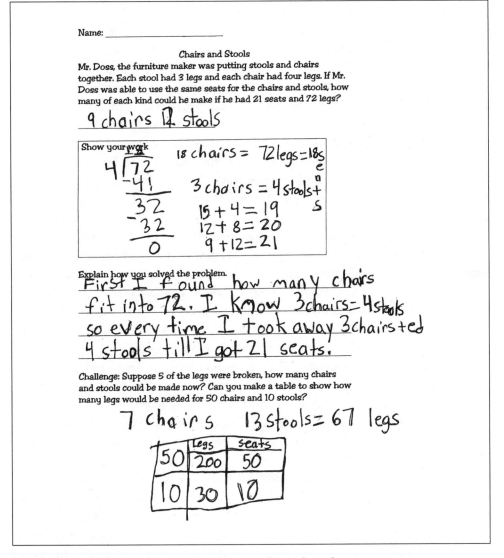

Name: _____

Chairs and Stools

Mr. Doss, the furniture maker was putting stools and chairs together. Each stool had 3 legs and each chair had four legs. If Mr. Doss was able to use the same seats for the chairs and stools, how many of each kind could he make if he had 21 seats and 72 legs?

9 chairs 12 stools

Show your work

$$4\overline{)72}$$
$$-4$$
$$32$$
$$-32$$
$$0$$

18 chairs = 72 legs = 18 seats

3 chairs = 4 stools + seats

15 + 4 = 19
12 + 8 = 20
9 + 12 = 21

Explain how you solved the problem.

First I found how many chairs fit into 72. I know 3chairs= 4stools so every time I took away 3chairs+ed 4stools till I got 21 seats.

Challenge: Suppose 5 of the legs were broken, how many chairs and stools could be made now? Can you make a table to show how many legs would be needed for 50 chairs and 10 stools?

7 chairs 13 stools = 67 legs

	Legs	Seats
50	200	50
10	30	10

Figure 6–1 *Jordon's work on the Chairs and Stools task*

without taking time to question his procedure, Mr. Cody wouldn't have had that insight into his thinking.

Interviews can be wonderfully enlightening and taking the time out of a busy schedule to meet one-on-one with students to discuss their work has huge payoffs in the end.

Performance-Based Tasks

Developing a good performance-based task is sometimes easier said than done. What we think will make a rich question for students to explore sometimes fails to address the mathematics as much as we would like. A performance-based task implies that we want the students to do something and we have identified a product that will serve as proof they have accomplished that task. However, doing an activity for the sake of doing an activity without attention to the mathematics involved is a waste of everyone's time. The first decision a teacher has to make in determining what type of activity to do is what the math is. The second decision must be about the best way to address the concept and whether or not students will be able to demonstrate their knowledge. Performance tasks are not easy to assess unless the teacher has thought through all of the steps prior to assigning them, and even then adjustments may need to be made once students start working. We sometimes get surprised when we see what students actually read into the problems. An effective task must be relevant to the math, be rich in context, and provide opportunities for students to display their level of thinking. Scoring that task can sometimes be done with a generic rubric or a task-specific checklist. Whatever the criteria, students should be made aware of the criteria prior to starting the task. If the intent of the task is to get at multiple representations of the problem, then that must be a part of the scoring criteria. Some teachers prefer to score tasks in a holistic fashion. That means that when they create their rubric or scoring checklist, the elements within the tool apply to the whole product rather than a single element. For example, in a holistic rubric, a teacher might identify three to four elements that can be scored. These elements would all be grouped together and they would apply to the entire performance, not to individual pieces of that performance. Elements might include items such as completing the task, demonstrating understanding, and showing appropriate representations. The degree to which the student accomplished these elements would then determine his score. In an analytic rubric, individual elements, and the degree to which they are each achieved, are scored separately. For example, did the student demonstrate understanding of the problem, and to what degree? Did the student make a plan to solve the problem, and to what degree? Whether holistic or analytic, the rubric needs to have as one of its elements descriptions of how the representations will be scored. An element on a rubric associated with representations might read: "Communicates thinking clearly, using appropriate words, computation, diagrams, charts, or other representations." If students know ahead of time that the representation element is equally as important as the answer, they can attend to that portion of their response. Rubrics used in scoring tasks need to be easy to apply, and the score should not be difficult to determine. The more opportunities students have to be assessed using a rubric, the more comfortable they'll become with the process. If a task-specific scoring tool is needed, you can create a checklist that resembles the rubric but has specific information about that one assignment.

CLASSROOM-TESTED TIP

Pinch Card Scoring

Use index cards and write the numbers 0, 1, 2, and 3 down the side. As you walk around the room and observe students at work either independently or in small groups, you can pinch a card next to the score you would give their work at that point and hand the card to the student or group. This way no other students become aware of the score and the student can get quick feedback on her efforts and adjust as necessary. You can also make cards for students so that they can self-score their efforts.

Portfolios—Collections of Student Work

Portfolios allow students an opportunity to showcase their work. They also provide teachers and parents with a picture album that summarizes a student's progress and efforts. Assessments should not be snapshots in time; rather, they should capture a student at various places along his learning continuum. By carefully structuring the collection of student work, a teacher can gather evidence of growth and information on how a student's mathematical thinking has developed. Portfolios of student work need to be structured from the start. It isn't enough to just ask students to put evidence of their work in a folder. Instead, we need to be clear in what type of work we are expecting students to submit. For that reason, it is important to list for students some of the criteria they need to consider as they select work samples. In the area of representations, we want the students to select work that shows both their thinking and their ability to use multiple representations. They need to include samples of work that show that they

- used pictures to help them reach a solution

- used graphic representations of the data (more than one sample)

- used words to explain how they developed their solution

- used words to justify why their solution was correct

- used a graphic organizer to illustrate a procedure

- used more than one representation to reach their solution

- worked with a group to solve a problem

If the criteria for assessing the portfolio collection are made clear to the students beforehand and they have a checklist of desired elements, they can begin assembling their work at the start of the school year and as they find better examples of a certain type of work, they can replace previous selections.

In Mrs. Waller's fifth-grade class, her students regularly update and add to their portfolio collections. She hands each one of them a criteria checklist at the beginning of the year and goes over how they are to select work samples for their portfolios. She also lists some required pieces, such as formative assessment samples and journal entries on certain topics. The students are ultimately responsible for the rest of the collection. At the end of the year, she has her students go through their portfolios one more time and review all of the pieces they have chosen. At that time she asks each student to select one piece of work that the child is most proud of creating, and she invites parents in for an afternoon of sharing portfolio samples. Parents first walk around the room, looking at the various pieces of student work, and then she has the students present their one sample that they chose from all of their work pieces. The students explain why this is a good work sample and what they have learned from the assignment, and then they show how the sample meets the criteria. This activity creates wonderful communication between students, the teacher, and parents, and at the same time it provides additional motivation for the students in making careful selections along the way, since they know their parents will be in to look through all of the samples. At the end of the gallery walk, Mrs. Waller encourages parents to take their child's collection of work samples and share it with the next year's teacher at an appropriate time.

Assessment Equity

With the growing trend toward full inclusion, teachers today have more challenges than ever in making sure students are assessed fairly and equitably. All students must be assessed. The question is How do you assess students with special needs and report their performance with clarity? In assessing representations, the answer may be a little easier than in other areas since alternative representations do in fact have a tendency to meet the needs of our special learners.

- *Provide a Frame or Context for the Problem:* Many of our lesson plans and assessment documents can be adapted so students can answer in an alternate form. For example, instead of asking a student to answer a question such as "Which is greater, four-fifths or five-fourths?" you can ask the student to place the two fractions on a number line. By asking the question in this manner and providing the number line, you present the student with a framework for the question, which may allow him to more easily determine which fraction is larger when considering their placement on a number line. You might also ask the student to represent the two fractions in a drawing, which would give you even more information about the child's understanding of the relative size of the two fractions.

- *Use Manipulatives:* Continue the availability of manipulatives during assessments. By making classroom tools available during assessment time, you help all students feel comfortable accessing them as they work through problems. The students can work the solutions out using the manipulatives and then make the appropriate representations on the paper.

- *Conduct Group Assessments:* Consider allowing students to take an assessment as a group. In this type of assessment, students will feel free to discuss the mathematics and also show each other how they would represent their ideas either pictorially or numerically.

- *Make Use of Technology:* There are a number of opportunities today to have students demonstrate their knowledge using technology. Teachers can make use of virtual manipulatives to help students solve problems and then have them translate the pictures to their own work.

Feedback

The purpose of assessment is to provide information, and that information needs to be used to inform instruction. What do we do with the evidence we collect on our students' performance? We can begin by asking questions about some of the student work we collect. Have the students communicated their solutions with appropriate words, numbers, and/or pictures? What mathematical thinking is evidenced in their work? What are some of the differences in the ways students found results? We also need to be mindful of the task we have given them and ask ourselves if it provided us with the information we thought it would or if we need to revise the task to make it richer. Do we have sufficient information on how the students have performed as compared with the standards, and if not, what do we need to do in order to help them improve? And finally, what information can we provide parents about their children?

Assessment is no longer about a grade, it is no longer about a moment in time, and it is no longer about just an answer without an explanation of process or justification for procedure. Assessment needs to be ongoing, it needs to be informative, and it needs to be accessible to all students. Having students skilled in solving problems using a variety of representation strategies is a goal that we all can set for ourselves and for our students. If we are to help our students grow in the math competencies, we need to provide them with as many strategies as possible along the way. We need to continue to look for and create those assessment items that allow our students multiple pathways to achieving success.

Questions for Discussion

1. What are some of the ways students can be assessed?

2. How can student interviews provide insight into our students' thinking?

3. What advantages can be found in using rubrics for scoring tools?

4. What feedback can we supply students about their assessment data?

5. How can the use of representations help in our assessment of special needs students?

7

Representation Across
the Content Standards

*Students in the elementary and middle grades use a variety of forms of
representation to record and communicate their thinking: symbols, drawings and pictures, tables and charts, physical materials, graphs, models,
and oral and written language.*

—Suzanne Chapin, Catherine O'Connor, and Nancy Anderson,
Classroom Discussions: Using Math Talk to Help Students Learn

We have been focusing on helping our students develop the ability to represent their
thinking and the mathematical concepts they are learning about. Being able to represent both externally and internally will enable students to approach novel situations
with many strategies from which to choose. Symbols, drawings and pictures, tables
and charts, graphs, manipulatives, models, and oral and written language are just some
of these representations. Representation, however, is only one of five different process
standards set forth by the National Council of Teachers of Mathematics (NCTM
2000). The other four include problem solving, reasoning and proof, communication,
and connections. Representation is interconnected to each of these other processes.
When problem solving, students might use representations in the form of pictures to
help them understand the problem, and then they might represent their solution in
the form of an equation. They use reasoning skills to infer and decipher information,
and they might use representations to justify their answer to a problem. To communicate their thought processes, students might create a representation in the form of
a diagram or an equation. Students connect math concepts to other math concepts and
to the world around them, and representations such as a graph or manipulatives can
help to show these connections.

Just as the process standards are interconnected, we must connect content to those process standards in a meaningful way. NCTM (2000) has outlined content standards in five areas: number and operations, algebra, geometry, measurement, and data analysis and probability. In this chapter, we look at how the use of representations can be developed and used across the content standards. In each section, we give an overview of a lesson or problem task related to the content standard, highlight the use of representation in the lesson or activity, and discuss the mathematics involved.

Number and Operations

Students who understand the structure of numbers and the relationships among numbers can work with them flexibly. (NCTM 2000, 149)

Students in grades 3 through 5 continue to develop number sense while working more with the concepts of multiplication, division, and rational numbers and their operations. As they grow in their understanding of these operations and become more fluent in using multiplication and division to solve a variety of problems, they begin to make generalizations that they can later apply when working with various operations involving decimals and fractions. The following activity was conducted in Mrs. Handy's fifth-grade math class and required students to apply a common problem-solving strategy, working backward, as they looked for ways to represent a tricky problem with fractions.

The Problem Task

A Bowl of Cherries

In the middle of the night, Linda's dad was so hungry he came downstairs and ate $\frac{1}{6}$ of the cherries her mother had put in a bowl. After that, her brother then came down and ate $\frac{1}{5}$ of the remaining cherries before going back to bed. Her sister came down, and you guessed it, she ate more cherries. In fact, she ate $\frac{1}{4}$ of the cherries left in the bowl. When Linda came down, she ate only $\frac{1}{3}$ of the remaining cherries. By the time Linda's mother came down the next morning, there weren't many cherries left. In fact, after she ate $\frac{1}{2}$ of the cherries, only 3 cherries remained in the bowl. How many cherries were in the bowl to start?

Mrs. Handy first let the students discuss the meaning of the problem in their cooperative groups and how they were going to tackle the problem. Since the problem was somewhat difficult, she had determined that the entire problem would be done in small groups instead of independently. The students had a number of manipulatives and tools at their disposal such as two-color counters, color tiles, dry-erase boards, one sheet of easel paper with chart markers, and a calculator. Each group was allowed to choose the manipulatives they thought would help them the most.

Tom's group decided to start by getting a calculator and dry-erase board. Since the calculator performed fraction operations, Tom said he thought this one was easy and he started adding $-3 + \frac{1}{6} + \frac{1}{5} + \frac{1}{4} + \frac{1}{3} + \frac{1}{2}$ while Maria wrote down the problem on the dry-erase board. The rest of the class was waiting for Tom to finish since there wasn't much need in continuing if he already had the solution figured out. When Tom finished his calculations he showed Maria the calculator and she wrote down the answer on the dry-erase board: $4\frac{9}{20}$.

Charlie was the first to speak up, saying that the answer wasn't right. "How can you have nine-twentieths of a cherry?" he asked. Suddenly everyone realized that Tom's method wasn't going to work and they headed to the manipulatives.

Brian's group opted for two-color counters, as did Ruth's, and Ann's group took the color tiles. Tom's group was still trying to figure out what they did wrong! Even with the manipulatives on the desk, students still weren't sure how to start. Many of them put three counters or tiles to represent the remaining cherries on their desk but did little else. Finally, in an effort to get everyone moving again, Mrs. Handy asked the groups to stop and reread the problem. Once everyone had read the problem, she asked, "What information are you being asked to find?"

Maria said that they were to find how many cherries were in the bowl before everyone came down to eat them. Mrs. Handy continued, "What information do you know about the cherries?"

Tom spoke up first this time. "We know only three cherries were left and everybody ate some."

Charlie continued, saying, "Her dad ate one-sixth of a cherry."

At this point Ruth countered with, "He didn't eat one-sixth of a cherry, he ate one-sixth of the cherries. That's a lot more than one-sixth of one cherry."

At this point Mrs. Handy had to decide whether she needed to continue to guide her students toward a solution or again let them work through the problem in their groups. She decided to let them continue working, but she did offer them a couple of pieces of advice. First she told them to try drawing some type of representation for the situation and then she suggested they look at working through the problem backward. She told them to start at the end of the problem rather than at the beginning. And with that she gave them the go-ahead to continue.

This time, each group set out to first draw a picture of what they thought the problem was asking of them and then model the problem with their counters or tiles. Maria was the first to comment that since there were only three cherries left in the bowl after Linda's mother ate half of the cherries, that must mean that three cherries was half of what was in the bowl when her mother came down that morning. Everyone was excited at this point because they finally had more whole numbers to deal with instead of just fractions. Maria's group drew their interpretation of that part of the problem; see Figure 7–1. The three cherries left at the end were one-half of the bowl's previous amount, which must be six.

With a solid start, the group continued to talk through the problem and draw the counters that they had on their desk. The next statement from the problem said that Linda ate one-third of the cherries. Brian's group was also ready to move on the next statement, and Brian offered that since there were six cherries left after Linda ate one-

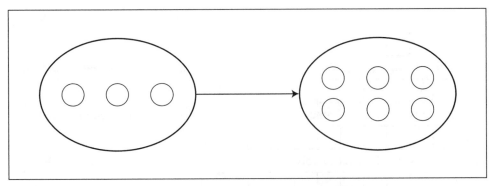

Figure 7–1 *Maria's group drew three cherries and six cherries to show the end of the problem.*

third, she must have started with nine cherries and also eaten three cherries. Charlie wasn't convinced. He asked, "How can one-half and one-third be the same number of cherries? Doesn't one-half have to be more?" Maria explained that this was possible because the number of cherries changed and one-half of six was the same number as one-third of nine.

The next part of the problem said that one-fourth of the cherries had been eaten by Linda's sister, which resulted in the nine cherries being left. Tom spoke up and said, "We know that if one-fourth of the cherries were eaten, then three-fourths were left and three-fourths of something is equal to the nine." While the students understood the concept of three-fourths remaining, they weren't quite sure how to set up the problem. As the groups continued to work through the problem, they discovered what they thought might be a pattern. Since one-half of the cherries was equal to three and one-third of the cherries was also equal to three, maybe three cherries got eaten every time. At this point they decided to test the pattern instead of continuing with the problem as they had done. Charlie's group drew the representation in Figure 7–2 with their color tiles.

Now that they had worked all the way back to the beginning, they decided to read through the problem and see if their solution made sense. So, with Maria pointing out the steps, Charlie read the problem again.

"Linda's dad ate one-sixth of the cherries and one-sixth of eighteen is three, so if there were eighteen cherries to start, eighteen minus three left fifteen cherries.

"Linda's brother ate one-fifth of the remaining cherries, and one-fifth of fifteen is three, and fifteen minus three equals twelve remaining cherries.

"Linda's sister ate one-fourth of the twelve cherries, and that is three, so twelve minus three equals nine cherries left.

"Linda ate one-third of the nine remaining cherries, and that is also equal to three, so now there are six cherries, and when her mother comes down to eat one-half of the cherries, she too only eats three."

Everyone applauded their efforts, but many were quick to say that they couldn't believe that all of those different fractions could equal the same amount.

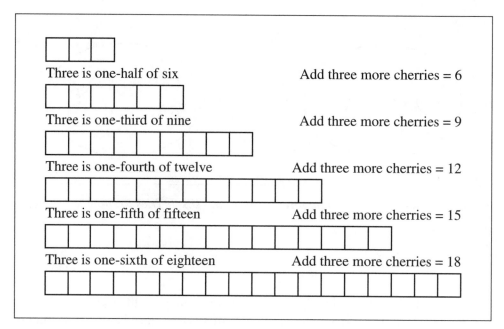

Three is one-half of six   Add three more cherries = 6

Three is one-third of nine   Add three more cherries = 9

Three is one-fourth of twelve   Add three more cherries = 12

Three is one-fifth of fifteen   Add three more cherries = 15

Three is one-sixth of eighteen   Add three more cherries = 18

Figure 7–2 *Charlie's group's representation*

About the Math

Problem-solving experiences with fractions allow students opportunities to clarify concepts and skills that are all too often forgotten when students fail to internalize the processes. Even though this problem was challenging for the students, the numbers were manageable, and as the students discovered, once the pattern was spotted, the whole problem became that much easier. Tom's insight into looking at the problem in terms of what was left when he indicated he knew three-fourths remained once one-fourth had been eaten, while accurate, didn't really help his group since they were unsure of how to set up the problem. Mrs. Handy decided to let them continue without stepping in because showing them how to set up the equation was not what she wanted them to get from this problem. As it turned out, they were able to solve the problem without the equation, and when their instruction gets them to the point of using equations, Mrs. Handy can always refer back to this situation.

In this problem, students started out by using a common tool that everyone thought would help with all math problems: the calculator. In this case, it might have helped if the students understood what numbers to input. But in this problem, they couldn't see the pattern in the solution until they started to draw it out while using the manipulatives. Students who learn early on that alternate methods of working through problems can sometimes be easier to use than a calculator will be able to apply those skills to more complex problems, provided they have opportunities to continue to practice those strategies.

The fact that representations are such effective tools may obscure how difficult it was to develop them and more important, how much work it takes to understand them. (NCTM 2000)

Purchase packages of inexpensive plastics cups in red, yellow, and green. When students are engaged in small-group work, give them a stack of three plastic cups, one of each color. As the students are working, they should have their green cup at the top of their stack. If they begin to experience problems along the way, they need to put the yellow cup on top. The yellow cup tells you that the students are having a little trouble but they are still working. With the yellow cup on top, students know to try to figure out how to continue without the teacher's help. The last resort is the red cup. When the red cup goes on top, it is a signal for the teacher that the group can't continue without assistance and they need help *now*. If cups aren't available, use laminated signs in red, yellow, and green that students can put on the corner of their desk. The cups reassure the students that they can ask for help but that they need to try to work things out first. The teacher is always the last resort.

Algebra

More and more teachers are being asked to foster algebraic thinking at all grade levels. The big ideas of algebra, including equivalence, properties, and variables, show up in primary classrooms today. When students think of algebra, they think of variables and the very abstract nature of the standard makes teaching it all that much harder. In order for students to understand the generalized nature of algebra, they need to see the connections to arithmetic at each grade level. For this reason, problems that provide students with opportunities to make those connections need to begin early.

The following activity, conducted in a fourth-grade class, involves figuring out two unknown quantities based on information given in the problem.

The Problem Task

The following problem was posed in a fourth-grade classroom to observe students' number sense, use of algebraic principles, and use of representation to solve the problem. Through this problem task, students were immediately engaged in exploring math content through the process of problem solving.

> Two apples and four grapes weigh eight ounces. Three apples and two grapes weigh ten ounces.
>> How much do seven grapes weigh?
>> How much do one apple and six grapes weigh?

In order to promote discussion about their thinking, the teacher, Ms. Sterling, asked students to work with a partner to complete the activity. After Ms. Sterling posed the problem and answered questions students had about it, the students got to work. Students had access to one-inch color tiles, paper, and pencils. While the students worked, the teacher circulated, listening to the children's conversations, questioning to promote thinking, and clarifying the task when necessary.

Initially, most of the students did not know where to begin with this task. Several of them attempted to add the different numbers in the problem, arriving at sums such as six (two apples and four grapes), five (three apples and two grapes), or eighteen (eight ounces and ten ounces). They did not understand the meaning of the task and applied operations that were erroneous and nonsensical. The teacher stopped the groups and posed the question, "What do we need to know before we can answer the two questions in the problem: How much do seven grapes weigh? and How much do one apple and six grapes weigh?"

After a moment of silence, Alvaro raised his hand and said, "We have to know how much one grape weighs."

Ms. Sterling responded, "Yes, and what else do we need to know?"

Ana raised her hand and said, "We also have to know how much one apple weighs."

Some of the students said, "Ohhh," indicating a new understanding, and got back to work.

One group of students got out some tiles to represent the apples and grapes. Juan selected two red tiles and four green tiles to represent the information in the first equation. Then he and his partner, Melissa, used a guess-and-check strategy to solve for the two unknowns. At first, they tried one ounce for the apple's weight and two ounces for the grape's weight. Pointing to each red tile, they counted by ones, and then pointing to each green tile, they counted by twos, but they discovered that using those weights would give a sum of greater than eight ounces in the first equation. Then Melissa said, "Wait. An apple weighs more than a grape, so let's try switching the two numbers." Giving the apple a weight of two ounces and a grape a weight of one ounce made more sense and worked numerically with the information given in the first part of the problem. Because these numbers worked with the first equation (two apples plus four grapes equals eight ounces), they were satisfied that they had solved for each unknown and used that information to answer the two questions in the problem. However, they did not test these numbers out in the second equation: three apples plus two grapes equals ten ounces. This was a common mistake that students made when solving this problem. In some cases, the students did check the numbers out in the second equation, but because they didn't work, they simply disregarded that piece of information, satisfied that the numbers they chose worked in the first equation.

One pair, however, came to the same initial conclusion (that one apple weighed two ounces and one grape weighed one ounce). They drew a picture of apples and grapes to test these numbers (see Figure 7–3). They soon discovered that those weights did not work in both equations.

They then adjusted the weights, keeping consistent the idea that the apples should weigh more than the grapes. Representing the apples and grapes with tiles, as mentioned earlier, they gave each apple a weight of three ounces. They first assigned

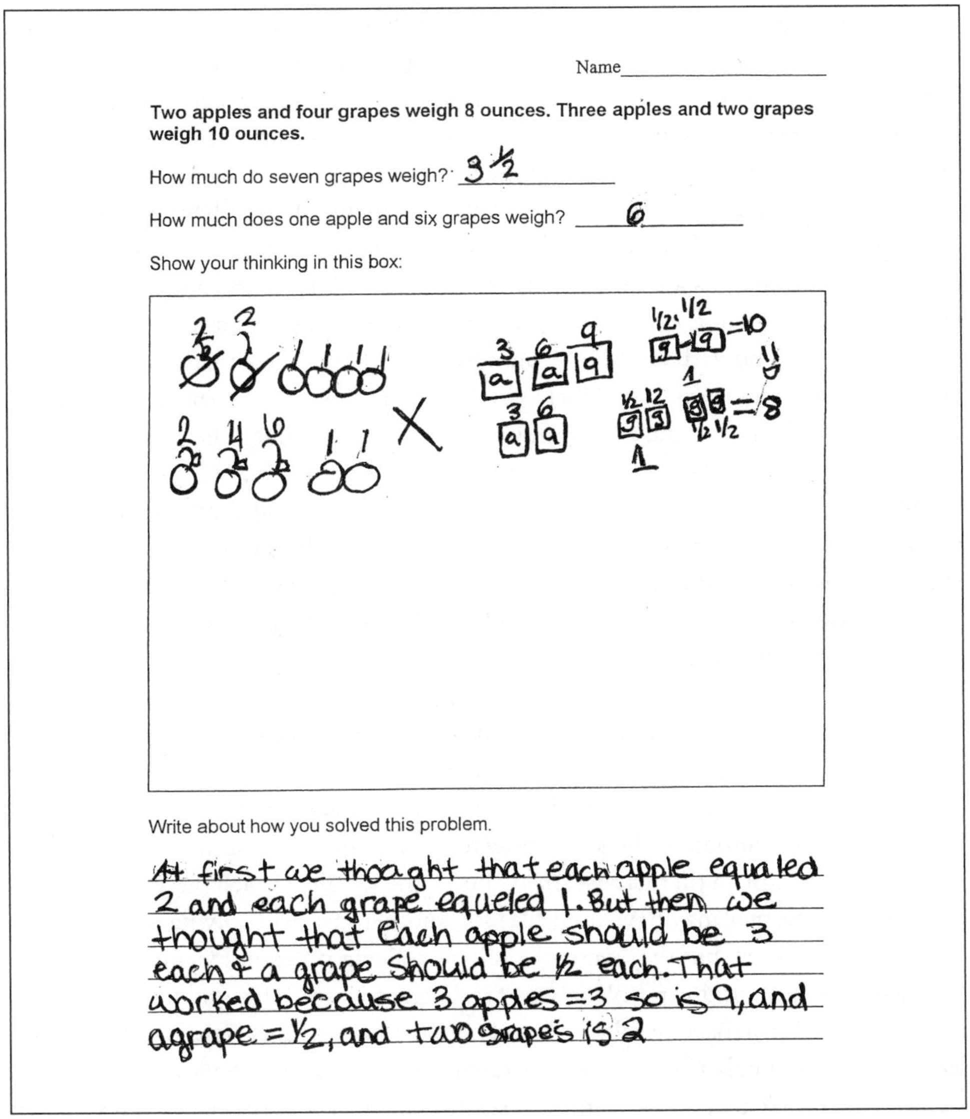

Name_____

Two apples and four grapes weigh 8 ounces. Three apples and two grapes weigh 10 ounces.

How much do seven grapes weigh? __3½__

How much does one apple and six grapes weigh? ___6___

Show your thinking in this box:

Write about how you solved this problem.

At first we thought that each apple equaled 2 and each grape equeled 1. But then we thought that each apple should be 3 each & a grape should be ½ each. That worked because 3 apples =3 so is 9, and a grape = ½, and two grapes is 2

Figure 7–3 *One pair tested their ideas by drawing pictures.*

a value of three to each of the two apples in the first equation, but became unsure of what to do with the remaining four grapes, so they looked at the second equation (three apples plus two grapes equals ten ounces). They assigned a value of three to each of the apples in that equation, giving them a subtotal of nine. They knew that for the equation to be true, the two grapes must together equal one. Quickly, Andrea said, "Each grape must be one-half because one-half and one-half equals one!" With this information, they tried out the first equation through tiles and discovered that those numbers would result in a true equation in that instance as well. Using additional tiles and applying those values, they determined that seven grapes must weigh three and a half ounces and one apple and six grapes weighed six ounces. These students were able to show their thinking with manipulatives, make a pictorial representation of their thinking, and explain their thought process in words.

One student, Alberto, initially appeared indifferent about the activity. He read it over and made the decision that he was not going to do it, perhaps because it was too difficult or because he didn't understand where to begin. The teacher encouraged him to discuss the problem with his partner, who seemed to be having difficulty as well. She then suggested that they use tiles to help them think about the problem. Alberto and Simi spent the remainder of the activity time manipulating the tiles in different ways, but not in ways that would help them solve the problem. They were unable to solve for the unknowns and did not get any of their thinking down on paper. However, when Ms. Sterling announced that it was time to regather and do some group sharing, Alberto shouted out, "No! I want to solve it! Don't tell me the answer!" Ms. Sterling didn't want to squelch Alberto's enthusiasm, but at the same time she didn't want to make the rest of the class wait while he worked through the problem. So she said to Alberto, "Alberto, I know you want to keep working, but we're running short on time. Would you be willing to come up to the overhead and show us how you are working to solve this problem?" He agreed, and Ms. Sterling assisted him in arranging the tiles on the overhead to represent the first equation. He then went through the same process that many of the other students did: assigning values, checking them out, and dismissing them when they didn't work. He determined the correct weights for the apples and grapes on his own, thinking out loud to share his processing with the class. The huge smile on his face when he finished solving the problem showed the pride and excitement he felt at his accomplishment.

The example of Alberto reminds us of several things. First, we cannot assume that students will automatically know how to use manipulatives and be able to assign some meaning to them (in this case, the value of the weight of each piece of fruit). Alberto and his partner may have used tiles for another problem-solving activity (such as area or perimeter), but they were not able to assign a different meaning to them as they worked through this problem. Ms. Sterling recognized this and helped Alberto arrange the tiles in a meaningful way based on what his thoughts were about the problem. She did not simply tell him how to arrange the tiles; rather, she allowed him to talk through the problem and together they used the tiles in a way that made sense to him and that would help him solve the problem. Second, Ms. Sterling faced a situation that many of us probably face during nearly every math lesson: students work at different paces and complete activities at different times, and therefore we must choose whether to press on or to give students the time they need (and deserve) to struggle with a concept. In this instance, Ms. Sterling's decision to continue the lesson *with* Alberto's help accomplished the goal of working within certain time constraints while recognizing Alberto's need for additional time and assistance in representing the problem. This allowed him, in a significant way, to solve the problem himself instead of being given the solution.

About the Math

This problem was rich because it included several different content and process standards. Students were challenged to use logic and reasoning to solve for the unknown quantities (the weights of the apples and grapes) in addition to number and operation skills to verify their answers. They used the NCTM (2000) algebra content standards of representing the idea of a variable as an unknown quantity using a letter or symbol and expressing mathematical relationships using equations. This was a multistep problem that required them first to solve for unknowns, then check that their solutions were valid (by making both equations in the problem true), and then apply what they knew to determine new information.

As the teacher helped Alberto record his thinking and solution to the problem, the students were able to see and hear a fellow student struggle as they had to arrive at the same solution. In addition, other students who might also have been confused about how the tiles would have been useful in solving the problem were able to see one use for them through Alberto's processing, and they also were able to see how the numerical symbols were related to the manipulatives.

In solving this problem, students were required to use their knowledge of operations, of equations, and of logic and reasoning to arrive at a solution that made sense. This problem was not easy for any of the students, yet nearly all of them were able to work through their processing with the use of representations and arrive at a common solution.

Geometry

> Geometry is a significant branch of mathematics, the one most visible in the physical world. (Burns 2002, p. 79)

Children have a natural curiosity about geometry. From an early age, they manipulate shapes, observing how they are similar and different, seeing how they fit together, and using them to create designs. They enjoy pointing out familiar shapes in their environment and experimenting with combining shapes to create new shapes. It is our role to help develop students' spatial abilities, and we should use varied experiences to help students connect geometry to ideas in number, patterns, and measurement. Students in grades 3 through 5 are moving beyond merely identifying shapes by name to more sophisticated ways of sorting and classifying shapes according to a shape's properties. They also are manipulating shapes, exploring the concepts of motion, location, and orientation. "The study of geometry in grades 3–5 requires thinking *and* doing" (NCTM 2000, 165). By embedding these experiences in problem-solving activities, we encourage students to investigate patterns in shapes and to use reasoning skills in a spatial context.

The Problem Task

The next task was posed to a fifth-grade class to observe their problem-solving skills, their understanding of fractions, and their ability to take a fixed area and divide it into fractional parts. After completing the activity with geoboards and geobands, students were asked to make a record (a more abstract representation) of their solution on geodot paper. Students had access to geoboards, geobands, pencils, and geodot paper to complete this activity. Before beginning this activity, the teacher, Mr. McRae, reviewed with the students the rules and expectations when using geoboards and geobands to help prevent off-task behavior. Together they quickly made a chart with the rules for the materials' use:

- Use the geobands as math tools, only to hook onto the pegs of the geoboard.

- Keep the geoboard flat on the desktop.

- Share geobands as necessary.

Once this quick review was complete, Mr. McRae presented the following problem.

Divide a 16-square-unit geoboard into fractional parts. You must include at least halves, fourths, and eighths. Make a record of your geoboard on geodot paper. Write number sentences to describe what you've shown with fractions.

The students were enthusiastic about this task because they enjoyed using the geoboards and the task was open-ended, with different possible solutions. They were instructed to complete it independently rather than work with a partner because Mr. McRae was interested in assessing individual understanding of the concepts presented in the task. They eagerly began working, attaching geobands to the pegs in different configurations. Mr. McRae quickly discovered, though, that there was some confusion about the directions. Many students were taking the geoboard, dividing it in half with a geoband, and then dividing one of the halves into fourths and then eighths. In essence, the students were changing what the whole was each time. Mr. McRae stopped the group and led a discussion on what the whole was (sixteen square units), and they discussed how the pegs on the geoboard represented the corners of the square that made up the whole. He reminded students to keep the whole in mind when they divided up the geoboard and that each fractional part must be a fraction of the *same* whole, sixteen units.

Mr. McRae circulated around the room while the students got back to work. Some students were still confused about the idea of the whole being constant, so he worked with individuals to clarify this concept. Many students found it easy to divide the geoboard in half (with a geoband vertically or horizontally in the center of the geoboard) but struggled with the other fractional parts. Still others were determined to solve the problem in a way that none of their classmates might think of. In Figure 7–4 we see a student who divided her geoboard in a nonsymmetrical way. When asked to prove that her board was indeed divided in half, she showed how she added up the whole squares and then the half squares (triangles) to get a total of eight square units on each side. She then went on to divide the rest of her board to show the remaining fractional parts, counting squares and triangles in each part to prove that it covered the correct area (i.e., four square units for one-fourth and two square units for one-eighth). Because her board was not divided into regular polygons, she spent quite a bit of time adding up the parts (squares and triangles) to ensure accuracy. Repeating this process with each fractional part helped to deepen her understanding of fractions and area and her spatial awareness.

Figure 7–4 *This student found an unconventional
way to divide her board in half.*

Some students created elaborate, symmetrical geometric designs on their boards, but when the teacher asked them to show how they had solved the problem task, their misunderstanding was evident. They subdivided each fractional part and thought that as long as somewhere in their design they showed each of the required fractional parts, they had succeeded in the task. Again, Mr. McRae clarified the directions of the task and nearly all the students were able to go on to finish it successfully.

Figure 7–5 shows a record of one student's work. This student divided up her geoboard using square units (rather than parts of square units, as described in the example earlier). Not only did she show halves, fourths, and eighths, but she also showed sixteenths. She then wrote number sentences at the bottom of the page that clearly showed her thinking, such as sixteen square units divided by two equals eight square units, or one-half of the geoboard. She then showed some knowledge of equivalent fractions (although the first one is inaccurate): four one-fourths are equal to one-half, and two one-eighths are equal to one-fourth. If asked to prove that four one-fourths were equal to one-half, it is likely that she would see her error and be able to correct it.

As students finished the activity, Mr. McRae directed them to prove to their neighbor that they had fulfilled the requirements of the task. By doing this, he was asking

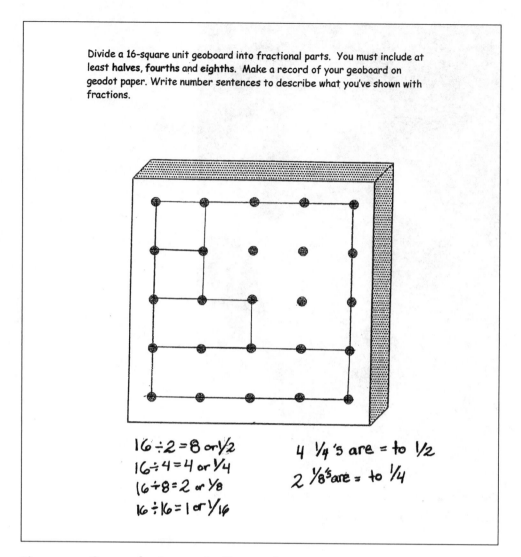

Divide a 16-square unit geoboard into fractional parts. You must include at least **halves, fourths** and **eighths**. Make a record of your geoboard on geodot paper. Write number sentences to describe what you've shown with fractions.

$16 \div 2 = 8$ or $1/2$
$16 \div 4 = 4$ or $1/4$
$16 \div 8 = 2$ or $1/8$
$16 \div 16 = 1$ or $1/16$

4 $1/4$'s are = to $1/2$
2 $1/8$'s are = to $1/4$

Figure 7–5 *One student's record of her work*

each student to justify her solution, and he was also exposing each student to at least one other classmate's way of solving the problem. At the conclusion of the math lesson, Mr. McRae directed half of the class at a time to circulate around the remaining half of the class to see how those students solved the problem and to ask questions about their solutions. They then switched and the other half of the class got a chance to share their solutions. Classmates made comments such as "Wow! I never thought of doing it that way!" and "Wait. How does this show one-half?" again requiring students to justify their thinking.

About the Mathematics

This task required students to draw on their knowledge of fractions and area and to use their spatial reasoning to solve a problem. The concept of halves, fourths, eighths, and in some cases, other fractions, was reinforced as students worked to divide their geoboards. They used such vocabulary as *horizontal, vertical, diagonal, symmetrical,* and *square units* as they described their solutions. Their confidence as young mathematicians was further developed as they went through the process of tackling a problem and then justifying their solutions to a peer.

In addition, students were asked to use visualization to solve this problem. While they had concrete materials to use, many of them pictured the fractional part in their heads (e.g., "I know that one-fourth of sixteen is going to be four square units.") before attaching the rubber band to the geoboard. NCTM (2000, 168) argues that students should not only study physical models of geometric shapes but also develop and use mental images. This activity helped in the development of that skill.

Measurement

Measurement is a process that students in grades 3–5 use every day as they explore questions related to their school or home environment. (NCTM 2000, 171)

Measurement, like geometry, is an area in which children have a natural curiosity. Even very young children enjoy using tools such as rulers and measuring tapes to measure the length of objects, and they experiment with different concepts in measurement, such as time: "I'm coming to your house at fourteen o'clock!" As children get older, their understanding of what it means to measure an object grows, and in grades 3 through 5, students' understanding of the use of measurement should deepen and expand. They begin to develop and use formulas to help them determine different measurements such as area and perimeter. Their concept of time is more realistic and they can apply their knowledge of time to different situations, such as how much time remains before lunch or how long it takes to get to Grandma's house. They also begin to have more of an appreciation for units of volume and have clear benchmarks in their minds, such as a gallon jug, a two-liter soda bottle, and a pint of milk. It is important for teachers at this stage to help students to connect ideas within measurement with other mathematical concepts and other disciplines, such as art and music.

In grades 3 through 5, students are learning about the concepts of area and perimeter. Through many varied and hands-on activities, students begin to deepen their understanding of these concepts and learn to correctly recognize when a situation involves area or perimeter, or both. In the following task, students were asked to apply what they knew about perimeter to create different shapes with the same perimeter.

The Problem Task

Before posing this task to her third- and fourth-grade students, the teacher, Mrs. Willingham, asked students what they knew about the concept of perimeter. Their responses included "It's like a picture frame" and "It's like running around the playground." It was obvious that this group of students had had experiences with perimeter as being the distance around something and could associate the concept with familiar objects and ideas. She then put a square tile on the overhead and asked a student to come up and show how he might find the perimeter of this object, which he did by counting up the sides around the shape. Then she made a shape with several tiles and asked another student to come up and demonstrate how to find the perimeter of the shape. Finally, she posed the task:

> **Draw three different shapes on centimeter-squared paper. You must follow three rules:**
>   1. **Stay on the lines when you draw.**
>   2. **If you were to cut out your shape, it must all be in one piece.**
>   3. **The perimeter of each shape must be 30 centimeters.**

To complete the task, the students had access to square tiles, centimeter grid paper, and pencils. Mrs. Willingham directed them to complete it independently but said they could ask a peer for assistance or clarification if they wanted.

The students were excited to begin working. Some students began drawing directly on the centimeter grid paper, but most of them found that it was an inefficient approach, as they had to erase to adjust their drawings to fit the rules given. One student, Marc, sat looking at the paper and tiles and didn't know where to start. Mrs. Willingham asked some questions to see where his confusion was. He said he didn't understand what he was supposed to do. After asking more questions, she realized that he did not have a good understanding of what perimeter was and therefore was unsure of how to create a shape with a perimeter of thirty centimeters. Mrs. Willingham took one tile and asked Marc to run his finger around the edges. She explained that that was the perimeter of the tile, or the distance around it. She then put two tiles together on the table and asked Marc to run his finger around the edge of the rectangle she had created. She again pointed out that he was running his finger around the perimeter of the shape. She then explained that we can assign numbers to figure out the distance around a shape. The single tile, for example, had a perimeter of four units because each side had a length of one. Running his finger around the four sides of the square tile, Marc could see that it was one plus one plus one plus one, equaling four units. Then Mrs. Willingham re-created the rectangle she had made earlier with two tiles and asked Marc to count the number of units around the shape. He used his finger to touch each side and determined that the perimeter was six units. She then asked him what it would mean to create a shape whose perimeter was thirty units, or in this case, centimeters. His response was that he would create a shape with tiles, and count each side on the outside of the shape, and it would have to equal thirty. Mrs. Willingham asked Marc to work on the problem for a few minutes by himself and said she would come back soon to see if he had any questions.

While she circulated to other students, she kept an eye on the progress Marc was making. He began by counting out thirty tiles and arranging them in such a way that sides were touching sides (i.e., there were no corners to corners), as shown in Figure 7–6.

He then counted up the outer sides of each tile in the shape and quickly discovered that his shape's perimeter far exceeded the required thirty centimeters. Frustrated, he messed up his shape and put his head in his hands. Mrs. Willingham quickly re-

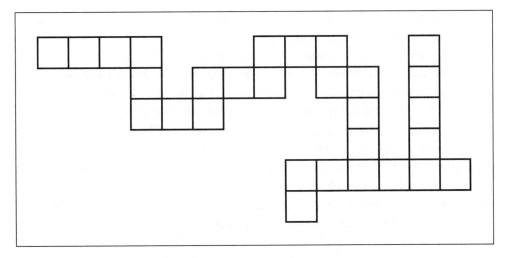

Figure 7–6 *Marc's first tile arrangement*

turned to him and asked him to explain what he had done. He said he had counted out thirty tiles, but that the perimeter was too much. Mrs. Willingham asked him if he thought he had to use thirty tiles to complete the task, and he responded that yes, he did think that. Again, she clarified that the perimeter had to be thirty centimeters, but that the area did not. She encouraged him to think about how he might adjust the number of tiles he used to create a shape with the target perimeter. He decided to go with a smaller number of tiles, fifteen. His new shape gave him a more reasonable perimeter (twenty-eight units), as shown in Figure 7–7.

Marc was pleased that he had gotten closer to the target perimeter, but he was now stumped about how to get two more sides. He added a tile to the end of the shape and was delighted to find that he now had the required perimeter of thirty centimeters. Mrs. Willingham pushed him to think deeper: How did adding a tile with four sides end up giving him a net gain of only two sides? She left him to think about it for a few minutes while she checked in with other students.

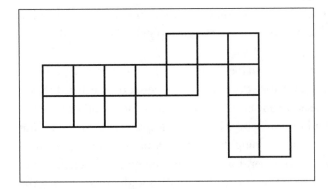

Figure 7–7 *Marc's second attempt*

Meanwhile, another student, Thomas, was struggling with the very same concept. He had also created a design with a perimeter of twenty-eight units. He knew he needed to somehow get two more sides. Experimenting with different placements of one tile, he was finally able to arrive at the target perimeter. When asked how he figured it out, he explained that he just kept moving the tile around and counting up the sides each time until he got thirty. Mrs. Willingham challenged him to think further. She took away the last tile added to his design and asked him what the perimeter was. He counted up each side again and answered that it was twenty-eight. She then slid the last tile into the location where he had placed it and asked him to think about just the outer sides of that tile and the outer one that was previously exposed in the shape but that was now touching the last tile added. He thought for a moment and then responded, "Before, this side was out and I counted it. Then I put this tile next to it, so now that side is covered, so I can't count it, and I lose one side. But adding this tile gives me three more sides that I can count. So even though I lost one side, I added three more, and I needed to add two more, so the one I lost is canceled out by one of the sides I added, giving me the two more sides that I needed." Tommy showed perseverance in justifying why his solution worked and demonstrated a deeper understanding of how the measurement of a figure's perimeter can be manipulated by changing its shape. Mrs. Willingham asked Tommy to sit by Marcus and ask him how this concept applied to the shape he had created.

One student was frustrated with her attempts to count up the perimeter of her shape. She kept losing track of where she had started and miscounted by either omitting some units or recounting others. Mrs. Willingham gave her a small counter (a paper clip or a bean would work as well) that she could place by the side where she started counting, and that helped her know where to stop.

Creating the shapes with tiles proved challenging for some students, but transferring the shape to centimeter-squared paper was even more challenging. In order to do it accurately, students needed to plan how much space they would need to transfer the shape. Some students simply began in a corner of the grid, but soon learned that part of their shape extended beyond the grid, and they ended up having to erase and start over. Mrs. Willingham asked them how they could use the tiles in their shape to know where to begin drawing on the paper. Shana replied that she could count up how many tiles "high" her shape was and make sure she had that many spaces going up and down on the paper in which to draw her shape. Vanessa added that she could count the tiles across her shape to get an idea of how much space across the grid she would need. Mrs. Willingham asked them to use their strategies to help them transfer their shapes to paper.

As students finished transferring their shapes to paper, Mrs. Willingham gathered the group to share out their thoughts about the activity. One student offered that it was much easier with the tiles because she could move them around and change her shape more easily than if she had drawn it on paper first. Marc raised his hand and said that he got what perimeter was after doing the activity. Vanessa shared that she'd had a hard time drawing her shape on paper, but that counting up the tiles helped her figure out how much space she needed on the grid. Mrs. Willingham concluded the lesson by sharing that she had seen the students show perseverance in staying with the task until they had completed it, even when parts of it proved challenging for them.

This multistep task required students to draw on their understanding of what perimeter is, their spatial awareness, and their developing understanding of how manipulating a shape can change its perimeter. Some students developed strategies for reaching the target perimeter, such as Tommy, who began to understand that adding a tile resulted in a loss of one or more sides in the original design but that there was sometimes a gain in the number of sides that offset it.

Students also used problem-solving skills to complete the task. If their initial approach proved unsuccessful, they were encouraged to think about how they could modify what they had started with to get closer to the target, as in Marc's case. They were also challenged to create a two-dimensional representation of their three-dimensional shape, a skill that is not easy for some students but that must be developed. Representation in the forms of tiles and drawings proved essential to completing this task successfully.

Data Analysis: Statistics and Probability

> Learning to interpret, use, and construct useful representations needs careful and deliberate attention in the classroom. (NCTM 2000, 207)

The purpose of data analysis is to answer an engaging question, a question that has real implications and one that can be answered by collecting, organizing, displaying, and interpreting data. Students in grades 3 through 5 should have multiple opportunities to interpret data and decide which data display to use. Only by using a variety of data displays that are both real and meaningful will students understand the factors involved in making those decisions. Because the very act of collecting data is the direct result of asking a question, that question occasionally leads to a prediction about the data results, which can take place prior to the data being collected but also after the data has been collected and analyzed. Before collecting data, the teacher might ask, "What do you think the data will show?" Or once the data has been collected, he could ask, "What do you think will happen next?" It is because of this close relationship that the terms *statistics* and *probability* are usually encompassed through the term *data analysis*.

Simulations involving probability have not always been prevalent in grades 3 through 5, and for that reason, little has been done in this area beyond activities dealing with what sums are more likely to come up when rolling two dice or flipping a coin one hundred times and seeing if you get an equal number of heads and tails. Issues dealing with probability are all around us and more and more curricula are elevating the importance of this topic within the data analysis strand. No longer is the topic of probability relegated to the end of the curriculum, where it may or may not be covered. Probability simulations are among the most meaningful activities for students and they are relatively easy to plan and fun to implement.

The following activity was conducted in Mr. Cuppett's fifth-grade classroom as a part of his unit on probability. Students were working on the idea of fairness as it relates to games of chance. Fairness in games is a pretty familiar topic for students, so it doesn't take much to get them engaged in the activity. Before starting the activity, Mr. Cuppett asked students to think about the topic of fairness and how that plays into games of chance. Several of the students talked about games they had played at carnivals and about their parents playing the lottery and how they thought some games couldn't be won. Steven said he had played a dart game at the fair and lost every time. Mr. Cuppett asked him if that was because of the way the game was set up or because of his dart-throwing skills. He then asked them to design a spinner that they thought could be used in a game for two people that would make the game completely fair. He further told them that this spinner needed to have more than two sections (he was trying to avoid the fifty-fifty split).

Several of the students got to work right away drawing their circles and dividing out the area for the spinner. Grace drew her spinner so that there were four sections, and she labeled them A and B; in fact, most students drew spinners similar to the one Grace drew. (See Figure 7–8.)

Once students had a chance to share their spinners and discuss issues related to fairness in games, Mr. Cuppett gave them their task.

The Problem Task

You and your partner are going to play a game using a spinner [see Figure 7–9]. The goal is to determine the fairness of the game. In this game, player 1 will have to pay player 2 $5.00 every time player 1 spins. When player 1 spins, player 2 will have to pay out the amount indicated on the spinner. You will play this way 10 times and then you will switch roles. Keep track of each of your 10 spins. Before you start, take a close look at the spinner and write down your prediction as to who you think will have more money at the end of 10 spins, player 1 or player 2.

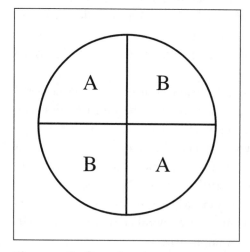

Figure 7–8 *Grace's spinner*

Mr. Cuppett gave the students an opportunity to read the problem and study the spinner on the overhead. Almost immediately James spoke up and said he knew right away that player 1 was going to make the most money. Rather than ask him to elaborate, Mr. Cuppett asked him to write down his thoughts about how he knew player 1 was going to come out ahead. Getting students to put their predictions down on paper prior to a simulation ensures they will be engaged in the activity because they have a stake in the outcome. Before the students set out to play the game, Mr. Cuppett asked for volunteers to raise their hand and share their prediction. Once again, James was the first to offer his guess that player 1 was going to be the big winner. This time, Mr. Cuppett asked him to explain why he thought this was so. James explained that player 1 was going to win because three of the four spaces had higher dollar amounts than the five dollars player 1 had to pay to spin, so naturally player 1 was going to make more money. Janine spoke up and said that she thought player 2 was going to win because the biggest area on the spinner was only three dollars, which meant that player 1 was going to lose two dollars a lot more often. Several other students spoke up with similar responses. Once the students had settled down and were ready to play, Mr. Cuppett passed out bags of play money and spinners along with tally sheets for students to keep track of their wins and losses, and everyone started to play.

Soon you could hear moans of disappointment when someone lost money, and there were the occasional cheers as money was won. Everyone was busy spinning and paying out money. At the end of ten spins, players switched roles and started their tallies all over again.

Mr. Cuppett had a large chart ready at the front of the room for students to record their final results. When students finished their second round of spins, they counted their tallies and wrote their final answers on the chart. When the class had finished their tallies, Mr. Cuppett totaled up the dollar amounts won or lost by both

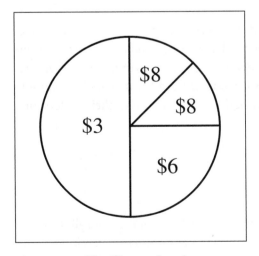

Figure 7-9 *Mr. Cuppett's spinner*

players, and while the chart did show that player 1 seemed to have a slight edge, the results did not have a large variance of dollar amounts. Before he allowed discussion of the results, Mr. Cuppett asked the students to go back to their predictions and compare them with the actual totals.

As the students settled down, Mr. Cuppett asked for comments. James again started off. "I thought player 1 would win by a much larger amount; maybe we just didn't do enough trials."

Steven replied, "Since we only have twenty-four people in the room, that's only twenty-four pieces of data. Don't we need more?"

As several students echoed the comments, Mr. Cuppett gave in and said, "OK, let's do one more round to see if we get anything different." Everyone cheered and started up again. Once again at the end of the trials the results were similar.

Mr. Cuppett could have given them a hundred more trials, but he knew what the results would be so he asked the students to look at the results and then at the spinner. By now Elliott had raised his hand and said, "When player 1 pays five dollars and lands on three dollars, he loses two dollars, right? And since three dollars is half of the circle, player 1 loses two dollars half of the time."

James picked up on the direction Elliott was heading and he said, "Player 1 wins three dollars when he lands on the two sections on the right and that is more than two dollars, so how come he doesn't win more?"

Grace then added, "He can't win more because the other half of that side only gives him one dollar, and that means that he wins three dollars half the time and one dollar half the time."

The students were beginning to see that even though the spinner looked like it wasn't fair, it actually caused player 1 to lose half the time and also win half of the time, and the amount was the same. The fact that there were four sections and only one section caused player 1 to lose didn't matter because that section was half of the spinner.

About the Mathematics

In this simulation, students were engaged in determining the fairness of a spinner game. By getting actively involved, the students had an opportunity to construct some of their own meaning as they worked through the task. By writing about their predictions and then comparing them afterward with the results, they had a chance to clarify their own thinking and the teacher had a better picture of their understanding of the concept of fairness.

Conclusion

Representations are useful tools for supporting children's learning across all the mathematical strands. By learning how to show their thinking, students are developing skills that will serve them well as they progress into more advanced mathematics. We should support this growth by providing students with many opportunities to experience math in a tactile as well as visual way, and by helping them to communicate their thinking through the use of manipulatives, pictures and diagrams, graphs, and numbers and symbols.

Questions for Discussion

1. In what ways can we connect the NCTM Content Standards with the Process Standards?

2. How did using tiles help students solve the first problem in this chapter, A Bowl of Cherries?

3. Some teachers argue that using manipulatives slows down the instructional process. What arguments can you give to help change their thoughts?

4. Using a table in the spinner problem helped students organize the data as they collected it. What are some other probability activities that our students would find interesting and that would encourage practice in using a table to organize data?

Accepting the Challenge

The Representation Standard

Principles and Standards for School Mathematics (NCTM 2000) describes representations as fundamental to understanding and applying mathematics. Representations give students a vehicle through which to process their thoughts, a mechanism to organize information, and an avenue for communicating about mathematics. The ways in which students use them give us, their teachers, insight into their level of understanding about various mathematical concepts, and they provide us with visual, hands-on ways in which to teach mathematics. In this book, we have discussed the importance of helping students learn to represent their mathematical thinking and ways in which they can do so. The very act of creating a representation of a concept helps to form an image of that knowledge in a student's mind and therefore a deeper understanding of that concept (Marzano et al. 2001). The goal of this book is to define what representations are, discuss the value in using them to explore mathematical topics, and illustrate how they might be used in a mathematics classroom. Through student work samples, examples of different representations, and activity suggestions, we hope to have made the case that the use of representations should be an integral component of any mathematics program.

Representations Support Learning

When students are learning to read, their teachers help them to develop a wide variety of strategies that will enable them to become confident, competent readers. Why should math be any different? Representation in math supports learning and helps students to develop a repertoire of strategies from which to pull when faced with novel tasks. For example, students who know how to use blocks to represent equal groups, a repeating pattern, or the value of a number have models in their minds that they can reconstruct or simply visualize when attempting to solve a new or challenging problem.

Students who are able to take a set of data and not only organize it into a chart or graph but also interpret it in a way to make meaning of it have skills that they can use when faced with new or large amounts of information. Students who can generate a picture to show their understanding of a problem and then use the picture to help them solve the problem own a strategy that they can choose to use in many different situations. In addition, students who can apply numbers and symbols in a meaningful way to simple or complex mathematical processes are making connections between the concrete and abstract. Representations really support and show evidence of learning!

Manipulatives in Different Forms

Manipulatives come in many different forms, both concrete and virtual, and provide both students and teachers with a means to model different mathematical concepts and processes. How can we expect students to understand the value of numbers if they are exposed to the numbers only in digit form? It is through building and manipulating concrete numerical representations that students begin to get a sense of how both small and large numbers can really be and what the digits in a number stand for. Using fraction circles or squares gives students a visual, concrete means to explore concepts such as one whole and one-half in addition to equivalent and nonequivalent fractions. How can we expect students to draw a representation of a fraction if they have not seen a perfectly proportioned one, as they would with fraction tiles? Manipulatives provide us with concrete, visual benchmarks of certain mathematical concepts, on which we can draw later.

Virtual manipulatives offer students and teachers additional experiences in representing mathematical concepts. There isn't the threat of running out of blocks, and students can print an instant paper copy of their representation. In addition, while some older students might find it juvenile to use blocks, tiles, and other concrete manipulatives, they are excited about manipulating images of those blocks on the computer. An interactive whiteboard provides a means for students to show their approach to solving a problem so that all their peers can see, which helps facilitate group discussion and strategizing. Technology is opening up a new world of possibilities for both teachers and students for exploring mathematical concepts.

We need to devote some time to thinking about which manipulatives we choose to use with our students, as different manipulatives can result in students constructing different understandings. Students whose early math experiences are with base ten blocks, for example, are more likely to develop a units view of numbers (such as hundreds, tens, and ones), while students who have many experiences with tools associated with counting, such as hundreds boards or number lines, are more likely to see the counting aspects associated with solving certain problems. Careful consideration about the influence manipulatives may have on students' understandings is a necessary part of the planning process.

Pictures and Diagrams

Pictures and diagrams are useful tools for young mathematicians as they attempt to create meaning from mathematical situations. They are a natural next step after manipulatives as students progress from the concrete to the abstract. As students deal with more and more complex concepts and larger numbers, they may find it necessary to rely on alternate representations, such as pictures and diagrams, as concrete manipulatives may become too cumbersome. It is important to stress, however, that this progression from the concrete to the abstract should occur when a child has a deep understanding of a mathematical concept and can communicate that understanding through concrete representations and words.

Pictures can give us great insight into a child's level of understanding about a concept. The ability to take the words from a math story or the numbers of a computation problem and create a visual representation in the form of a picture requires an understanding of the problem at hand. We can use the information we gain from studying children's pictorial representations to make instructional decisions that will meet their needs. Similarly, students can use the pictures or diagrams they create to help them communicate their thinking to others. It is oftentimes much easier for a student to talk about a picture she has created to process a problem than it is to explain in words alone how she solved it. Working with our students to become proficient and efficient in creating pictorial representations should be one of our goals as we help to develop our students' mathematical abilities.

Diagrams, like pictures, provide students with another way to show understanding. Venn diagrams are extremely useful in helping organize students' thoughts about similarities and differences between two or more objects or concepts. We must be sure to include activities with graphic organizers such as Venn diagrams, flowcharts, and T-charts to help students develop these comparison skills. Being able to compare and contrast requires high-level thinking at the analytical level, which leads to deeper understandings.

Numbers and Symbols

Just as students progress from concrete manipulatives to pictorial representations, they then progress to perhaps the most abstract form of representation: numbers and symbols. As students mature in their mathematical understandings, they reach a point where they are ready to learn about the numbers and symbols associated with concepts and processes. Timing is very important: to introduce the abstract too early may result in shutting down the meaning- and sense-making processes in children, and they may become overly concerned with memorizing procedures and formulas rather than thinking about the mathematics involved in a situation. An important role of the teacher is to be attuned to each child's level of understanding at the concrete level *before* attempting to introduce numbers or symbols.

Once students have demonstrated a deep understanding of a mathematical concept, we have to be sure that students then develop a deep understanding of the numbers and symbols they will be using. It is absolutely essential that there is no confusion about what the equals sign means. We need to assess our students' understanding of this very basic and important element of an equation and clear up any misunderstandings that may exist. Without this fundamental knowledge, equations have little meaning to students, and as they progress in higher-level mathematics, the holes in their understandings will grow.

Invented algorithms are wonderful windows into a child's mind. Their unique ways of interpreting a problem and applying their own understandings to its solution provide us with a good idea of what their level of understanding is and if there are any misconceptions. The invented procedures can also show us how students think about numbers. For example, if, when faced with a multidigit multiplication problem, a child breaks up the numbers into units, finds partial products, and then combines the parts to get a total, we can feel somewhat confident that the child has an understanding of place value and what the different steps in such a problem really mean. Information like this is invaluable as we plan experiences that will challenge our students and will also allow them to draw on their current understandings about different concepts.

Tables and Graphs

The purpose of graphing is to organize data in a meaningful display in order to make analysis of data easier. With this in mind, we need to plan meaningful experiences with graphing for our students. It is not enough to simply hand them a set of numbers and ask them to create a bar graph. Little understanding is developed through this passive approach to working with data. Rather, we need to think about graphing data with a purpose in mind: to answer a question that we or our students have posed and about which data has been collected. Then, after the data has been displayed on the appropriate type of graph, we must use it to answer the question originally posed.

Many of us spend too much time on ensuring that our students know how to label a graph correctly and not enough time on helping students to think about which graph would be most appropriate to display a set of data. Students need many experiences with different types of graphs so that they become familiar with their purposes and can make appropriate choices about which graph would be best for the task at hand. For example, students who choose to display the number of shoppers at a mall over an eight-hour period on a bar graph are not showing a deep understanding of the purpose of a bar graph or of the data itself. A line graph would be more appropriate for this type of data, and unless we give students many experiences creating and analyzing line graphs, they will probably not be able to correctly assign a line graph to a certain situation.

In addition to bar and line graphs, students in grades 3 through 5 should be familiar with line plots, circle graphs, double-line graphs, double-bar graphs, stem-and-leaf plots, and box-and-whisker tables. They need to do more than just see them and hear about them; they need to create them using meaningful data and analyze them. Bulletin boards are wonderful ways to display large graphs of different types. They are visible to the whole class and they can be analyzed by the whole group, small groups, or individuals. In the five minutes before lunch or dismissal, you can ask students to generate some true statements about the data on the graph. Two different graphs displayed side by side can serve as an opportunity to compare and contrast the two methods of displaying data and can serve as a discussion point about why each graph was chosen for the data it represents. Large visuals such as these can also allow for whole-group discussion about the shape of the data and about generalizations that can be made regarding the information displayed.

Graphing data is a wonderful tool for cross-curricular and multicultural activities and should be an integral part of our students' learning. With the vast resources available to us such as the Internet, newspapers, textbooks, and people around us, students should have many opportunities to think about topics that interest them and then be able to research those topics to collect data and organize the data in an appropriate display. This active engagement in data analysis will help our students to develop their critical and analytical skills with tasks that have meaning and are of interest to them.

Assessing Students' Representations

One of the more challenging aspects of a teacher's work is assessing student progress. Traditionally, the purpose of assessing students was to give teachers data in order to assign a grade. Fortunately, we use assessments for more meaningful purposes now, although we often still attach a grade to student performance. Assessment takes many forms, both formal and informal, and can be used to inform instruction, help students think about their learning, help parents understand their child's progress, and, most importantly, give us information about a child's level of understanding.

When faced with the task of assessing students' representations, we need to consider the purpose for which we are assessing. Is it to get a quick idea of whether or not a student understands a concept? Are we looking for mastery of a concept or skill? Are we looking for developmental growth in their use of representation? Depending on the desired outcome of the assessment, we have several different options. We might simply listen in to a conversation between two students as they work together to solve a problem, making anecdotal notes as necessary. Or we might assign a performance-based assessment, asking students to represent a concept in a way that makes sense to them. We might also assign a task and collect paper copies of the representations the students did, analyzing them at a later time, perhaps using a rubric. Or we may just ask a student to explain what he is thinking about a particular problem. Each of these forms of assessment can help us as we plan meaningful mathematical experiences for our students.

How Classroom Teachers Can Make This Work

As teachers, we often have the most control over our students' immediate learning environment. We spend much time planning the layout of the room, the correct seating arrangement to ensure collaborative work, and the right displays for the walls to help the room seem inviting and comfortable for our students. In most classrooms, there is a library that is visible and accessible to the students, but are there math tools in a visible and accessible location? Do we have number lines, graphics, and other mathematical representations hanging in our room to help support our students' learning in math as we do in language arts? A wonderful compliment for us to receive as teachers is that we have as much numeracy visible in our room as we do literacy. We must strive to balance our efforts in all areas of the curriculum and to include as many mathematical displays as we do reading displays.

Having math tools in a visible and accessible location sends the message to our students and others that math is important and that we will use whatever tools are necessary to help us to develop our mathematical thinking. Baskets of base ten blocks, linking cubes, counters, pattern blocks, rulers, string, markers, grid paper, and calculators, just to name a few, are some of the tools we want to provide our students the opportunity to use. Because math manipulatives can get expensive, one way to build up our classroom supply is to solicit some from our students' parents and our colleagues. There are many items in our homes that can serve as math manipulatives, such as coins, beans, toothpicks, craft sticks, ribbon, and containers, and parents are usually more than happy to help out by sending them in. We just have to ask!

One of the most important ways in which we can help to develop our students into competent and confident mathematicians is to become competent and confident mathematicians ourselves. It is not enough to rely on the math we learned in elementary school. A quick survey of our colleagues will likely show that the way they learned math was not a process of concept development and understanding, but rather a process of memorizing algorithms and procedures and doing as they were told. Fortunately, that approach to mathematics instruction is no longer the norm. However, that places a new challenge on us to go back and develop a deep understanding of the mathematical concepts we experienced only superficially when we were in school. Community colleges, local universities, and district-provided professional development offer ways in which we can relearn the math that we will be teaching our students. Without this strong content knowledge, it is difficult to analyze our students' representations to determine their level of understanding about a concept and then to determine the next steps to further their growth. It is only through having a deep understanding of the mathematics ourselves that we will be able to anticipate misconceptions by our students and to push our students to think more deeply about mathematics.

How School Administrators Can Make This Work

While classroom teachers have the most direct impact on students' learning, there are many ways in which school administrators can help to support them in this task. First, they can allocate funds to purchase high-quality math materials, such as base ten blocks, pattern blocks, geometric solids, fraction circles or squares, tiles, geoboards, and Cuisenaire rods, as well as invest in technology that will support student representations, such as software and interactive whiteboards. While it would be wonderful for there to be a class set of manipulatives in each room, at the minimum there should be one set for every two classrooms to share. Second, administrators can work with teachers and specialists to set up the master schedule so that team members have time to collaborate and talk about the mathematics they are teaching, and to actually experience concepts and activities *before* introducing them to the students. This is one of the best means for anticipating student misconceptions and planning appropriate responses to them. Finally, administrators can support professional development that will enhance their teachers' math content knowledge. This can be done by paying for teachers to attend math content classes, inviting a math consultant to come to the school, and purchasing teacher resources such as books and materials. School administrators are the instructional leaders in the school. By modeling a learning spirit, they encourage their teachers to further develop themselves.

Another way in which administrators can help students deepen their mathematical understandings through representations is by displaying representations around the school. With the help of the student council association, they can conduct a survey of students to learn about their suggestions for spirit days throughout the year. The data can be compiled into a graphical display that can be posted in the main hall (or outside the gymnasium, where there always seems to be some downtime!) or other central location where children will be able to see it, think about it, and discuss it. Another suggestion is to work with the school librarian to display information about types of books checked out by grade level. Again, student representatives could help in creating the data display. Aside from graphical representations, administrators can support the display of visual representations around the school by encouraging classroom teachers to hang outside their rooms student-generated examples from completed class activities, such as Venn diagrams or representations of sorted polygons. By communicating the message through words and actions that mathematical learning is important and valued, administrators can support teacher efforts to develop competent, confident mathematicians.

The Challenge to Teachers

We are entering a new and exciting era of teaching and learning mathematics, one that challenges students to explore, struggle with, and create their own understandings of mathematical concepts. Students are no longer handed knowledge through formulas or algorithms, but instead develop their own knowledge as a result of firsthand experiences. To meet this challenge, we must be willing to rethink the way we approach mathematics instruction. We must begin to view ourselves as experts in the content we teach, and as such, we need to do whatever it takes to become an expert: take a math content course, engage in regular dialogue with our colleagues about the math we teach, attend professional development seminars, and so on. In order to be able to help our students to think deeply about the mathematics they are learning, we must also think deeply about it.

The use of representations provides a particularly exciting opportunity to begin to think in more depth about math content. How will we use manipulatives to get children to think about the magnitude of a number? How will we show in pictorial form the meaning of a math story? In what ways can we use numbers and symbols to synthesize our thinking? These are questions we must ask of ourselves at the same time that we are asking our students to represent their thinking. It is a wonderful, exciting time to be a math teacher, and to meet the challenge of preparing our students to become confident, competent mathematicians, we must also become the same.

Questions for Discussion

1. What are the most important pieces of knowledge you have gained from reading this book?

2. What are ways in which teachers can support an environment that values mathematical representations?

3. What are ways in which administrators can support an environment that values mathematical representations?

4. How will you change aspects of your instructional planning to ensure that you give deep thought to the mathematics before introducing it to students?

The following resources are meant to support you as you continue to explore the representation standard in grades 3 through 5. You will find a variety of text resources—books that will provide you with additional activities and instructional strategies that will encourage student representations. A list of math-related literature books and math websites are included to supply you with classroom tasks, electronic manipulative ideas, and teacher resources.

Text Resources

The following text resources provide a variety of activities and strategies for supporting students as they develop their skills in representing mathematical thinking.

Andrini, B. 1991. *Cooperative Learning and Mathematics*. San Juan Capistrano, CA: Resources for Teachers.

Bender, W. 2005. *Differentiating Math Instruction: Strategies That Work for K–8 Classrooms*. Thousand Oaks, CA: Sage.

Bosse, N. R. 1995. *Writing Mathematics*. Chicago: Creative.

Burns, M. 1992. *The Way to Math Solutions*. Sausalito, CA: Math Solutions.

———. 2002. *About Teaching Mathematics*. Sausalito, CA: Math Solutions.

Burns, M., B. Tank, and T. Stone. 1988. *A Collection of Math Lessons, Grades 3–6*. Sausalito, CA: Math Solutions.

Countryman, J. 1992. *Writing to Learn Mathematics*. Portsmouth, NH: Heinemann.

Kagan, S. 1992. *Cooperative Learning*. San Clemente, CA: Resources for Teachers.

McIntosh, M., and R. J. Draper. 1997. *Write Starts*. New York: Dale Seymour.

Miller, E. 2001. *Read It! Draw It! Solve It!* Parsippany, NJ: Dale Seymour.

National Council of Teachers of Mathematics. 1989. *Curriculum and Evaluation Standards for School Mathematics*. Reston, VA: Author.

———. 1991. *Professional Standards for Teaching Mathematics*. Reston, VA: Author.

———. 1995. *Assessment Standards for School Mathematics*. Reston, VA: Author.

———. 2000. *Principles and Standards for School Mathematics*. Reston, VA: Author.

———. 2006. *Curriculum Focal Points for Prekindergarten Through Grade 8 Mathematics*. Reston, VA: Author.

125

Newman, V. 1994. *Math Journals*. San Diego: Teaching Resource Center.

O'Connell, S. 2001a. *Math—The Write Way for Grades 2–3*. Columbus, OH: Frank Schaffer.

———. 2001b. *Math—The Write Way for Grades 4–5*. Columbus, OH: Frank Schaffer.

———. 2005. *Now I Get It: Strategies for Building Confident and Competent Mathematicians K–6*. Portsmouth, NH: Heinemann.

Stewart, K., K. Walker, and C. Reak. 1995. *Thinking Questions for Pattern Blocks, Grades 1–3*. Chicago: Creative.

Van de Walle, J. A., and L. H. Lovin. 2006. *Teaching Student-Centered Mathematics, Grades 3–5*. New York: Pearson Education.

Whitin, P., and D. Whitin. 2000. *Math Is Language Too: Talking and Writing in the Mathematics Classroom*. Urbana, IL: National Council of Teachers of English.

———. 2003. *A Mathematical Passage: Strategies for Promoting Inquiry in Grades 4–6*. Portsmouth, NH: Heinemann.

Zikes, D. 2003. *Big Book of Math K–6*. San Antonio: Dinah-Might Adventures.

Math-Literature Connections

One of the ways teachers can help students learn how to represent their mathematical thinking is by using literature books to anchor an activity or lesson. There are an increasing number of books on the market today designed to link math and reading.

Adler, D. 1998. *Shape Up! Fun with Triangles and Other Polygons*. New York: Holiday House.

Anno, M. 1983a. *Anno's Magic Seeds*. New York: Putnam.

———. 1983b. *Anno's Mysterious Multiplying Jar*. New York: Philomel.

Axelrod, A. 2000. *Pigs at Odds*. New York: Simon and Schuster.

Barrett, J. 1978. *Cloudy with a Chance of Meatballs*. New York: Aladdin.

Burns, M. 1994. *The Greedy Triangle*. New York: Scholastic.

———. 1997. *Spaghetti and Meatballs for All! A Mathematical Story*. New York: Scholastic.

Caple, K. 1985. *The Biggest Nose*. Boston: Houghton Mifflin.

Cushman, J. 1991. *Do You Wanna Bet?* New York: Clarion Books..

Dahl, R. 1982. *The BFG*. New York: Puffin.

Gold, K. 1998. *Numbers Every Day*. New York: Newbridge Educational Publishing.

Hutchins, P. 1986. *The Doorbell Rang*. New York: Mulberry.

Lasky, K. 1994. *The Librarian Who Measured the Earth*. Boston: Little, Brown.

Neuschwander, C. 1997. *Sir Cumference and the First Round Table: A Math Adventure*. Watertown, MA: Charlesbridge.

———. 1998. *Amanda Bean's Amazing Dream: A Mathematical Story*. New York: Scholastic.

Pallotta, J. 1999. *Hershey's Fraction Book*. Hershey's Food. New York: Scholastic.

Pollack, P., and M. Belviso. 2002. *Chickens on the Move*. New York: Kane.

Schlein, M. 1996. *More Than One*. New York: Greenwillow .

Schwartz, D. 1997. *How Much Is a Million?* New York: Mulberry.

———. 1999. *On Beyond a Million*. New York: Random House.

Scieszka, J., and L. Smith. 1995. *Math Curse*. New York: Viking.

Silverstein, S. 1974. *Where the Sidewalk Ends*. New York: HarperCollins.

Websites

The following websites provide ideas and activities to use with students in helping them represent their math thinking.

> www.ics.uci.edu/~eppstein/numth/egypt/—This site, by Dr. David Eppstein of the University of California at Irvine, gives a summary of how Egyptian fractions were used and some examples of unit fraction sums.
>
> www.mcs.surrey.ac.uk/Personal/R.Knott/Fractions/egyptian.html—Rob Knott's teacher-friendly web page on Egyptian fractions with links to other sites on similar topics.
>
> www.mathcats.com/explore/oldegyptianfractions.html—This kid-friendly website, called Math Cats, has a section on Egyptian fractions.
>
> www.maa.org/editorial/mathgames/mathgames_07_19_04.html—The Mathematical Association of America's website on Egyptian fractions.
>
> regentsprep.org/Regents/mathb/2B2/algfracteacher.htm—The Oswego City School District's page on Egyptian fractions.

Stem-and-Leaf Plots

> regentsprep.org/Regents/Math/data/stemleaf.htm—This is a short tutorial on stem-and-leaf plots from the Oswego School District.
>
> www.purplemath.com/modules/stemleaf.htm—From Purplemath, this site shows some of the connections between stem-and-leaf plots and histograms.
>
> www.mathsrevision.net/gcse/pages.php?page=10—Provides examples of stem-and-leaf plots and other statistical models.

Rubrics

There are several great websites for making rubrics or using ready-made rubrics.

> rubistar.4teachers.org/index.php
>
> www.teach-nology.com/web_tools/rubrics/
>
> www.teachervision.fen.com/teaching-methods/rubrics/4521.html
>
> www.education-world.com/a_curr/curr248.shtml

Other Resources

> www.nctm.org—The National Council of Teachers of Mathematics websites

Bender, W. 2005. *Differentiating Math Instruction: Strategies That Work for K–8 Class-rooms*. Thousand Oaks, CA: Sage.

Bosse, N. R. 1995. *Writing Mathematics*. Chicago: Creative.

Burns, M. 1987. *A Collection of Math Lessons, from Grades 3 Through 6*. Sausalito, CA: Math Solutions.

———. 1992. *The Way to Math Solutions*. Sausalito, CA: Math Solutions.

———. 2002. *About Teaching Mathematics*. Sausalito, CA: Math Solutions.

Fisher, S., and C. Hartmann. 2005. "Math Through the Mind's Eye." *Mathematics Teacher* 99(4): 246–50.

Hatfield, M. 2004. *Mathematics Methods for Elementary and Middle School Teachers*. Hoboken, NJ: John Wiley.

Hiebert, J., T. Carpenter, E. Fennema, K. Fuson, D. Wearne, H. Murray, A. Olivier, and P. Human. 1997. *Making Sense*. Portsmouth, NH: Heinemann.

Hiebert, J., R. Gallimore, H. Garnier, K. Bogard Givvin, H. Hollingsworth, J. Jacobs, A. Miu-Ying Chui, D. Wearne, M. Smith, N. Kersting, A. Manaster, E. Tseng, W. Etterbeek, C. Manaster, P. Gonzales, and J. Stigler. 2003. *Teaching Mathematics in Seven Countries: Results from the TIMSS 1999 Video Study* (NCES 2003–013 Revised). Washington, DC: U.S. Department of Education, National Center for Education Statistics.

Hutchins, P. 1986. *The Doorbell Rang*. New York: Scholastic.

Marzano, R., D. Pickering, and J. Pollock. 2001. *Classroom Instruction That Works*. Alexandria, VA: Association for Supervision and Curriculum Development.

Moyer, P., J. Bolyard, and M. Spikell. 2002. "What Are Virtual Manipulatives?" *Teaching Children Mathematics*. Reston, VA: NCTM.

National Council of Teachers of Mathematics (NCTM). 1989. *Curriculum and Evaluation Standards for School Mathematics*. Reston, VA: NCTM.

———. 2000. *Principles and Standards for School Mathematics*. Reston, VA: NCTM.

Nolan, H. 2001. *How Much, How Many, How Far, How Heavy, How Long, How Tall Is 1,000?* Toronto: Kids Can Press.

Pallotta, J. 2003. *Count to a Million*. New York: Scholastic.

Parke, C., S. Lane, E. Silver, and M. Magone. 2003. *Using Assessment to Improve Middle Grades Mathematics Teaching and Learning*. Reston, VA: NCTM.

Sharp, J., and K. Hoibert. 2005. *Learning and Teaching K–8 Mathematics*. Boston: Pearson Education.

Schwartz, D. 1993. *How Much Is a Million?* New York: Mulberry Books.

130

References

Stewart, K., K. Walker, and C. Reak. 1995. *Thinking Questions for Pattern Blocks, Grades 1–3*. Chicago: Creative.

Van de Walle, J. A., and L. H. Lovin. 2006. *Teaching Student-Centered Mathematics, Grades 3–5*. New York: Pearson Education.

Why Are the Activities on a CD?

At first glance, the CD included with this book appears to be a collection of teaching tools and student activities, much like the activities that appear in many teacher resource books. But instead of taking a book to the copier to copy an activity, with the CD you can simply print off the desired page on your home or work computer. No more standing in line at the copier or struggling to carefully position the book on the copier so you can make a clean copy. And with our busy schedules, we appreciate having activities that are classroom ready and aligned with our math standards.

You may want to simplify some tasks or add complexity to others. The problems on the CD often include several parts or have added challenge extensions. When it is appropriate for your students, simply delete these sections for a quick way to simplify or shorten the tasks. Remember to rename the activities when saving to preserve the integrity of the original activities.

Editing the CD to Motivate and Engage Students

Personalizing Tasks or Capitalizing on Students' Interests

The editable CD provides a quick and easy way to personalize math problems. Substituting students' names, the teacher's name, or a favorite restaurant, sports team, or location can immediately engage students.

You know the interests of your students. Mentioning their interests in your problems is a great way to increase their enthusiasm for the activities. Think about their favorite activities and simply substitute their interests for those that appear in the problems.

One teacher knew that many of her students were interested in sports, so she decided to reword the following task to capture their interest. Note: This type of editing is also important when the problem situation may not be culturally appropriate for your students (e.g., your students don't play musical instruments or have 4-H clubs in their area).

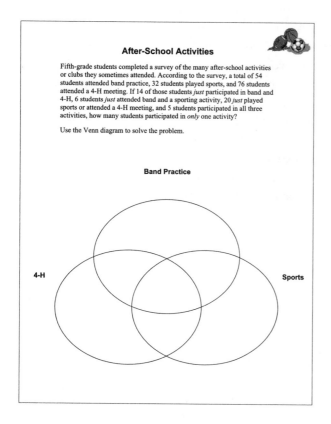

After-School Activities

Fifth-grade students completed a survey of the many after-school activities or clubs they sometimes attended. According to the survey, a total of 54 students attended band practice, 32 students played sports, and 76 students attended a 4-H meeting. If 14 of those students *just* participated in band and 4-H, 6 students *just* attended band and a sporting activity, 20 *just* played sports or attended a 4-H meeting, and 5 students participated in all three activities, how many students participated in *only* one activity?

Use the Venn diagram to solve the problem.

Band Practice

4-H

Sports

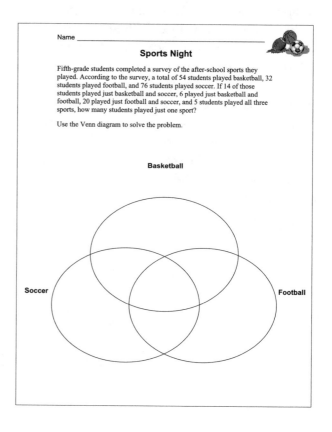

Name _____

Sports Night

Fifth-grade students completed a survey of the after-school sports they played. According to the survey, a total of 54 students played basketball, 32 students played football, and 76 students played soccer. If 14 of those students played just basketball and soccer, 6 played just basketball and football, 20 played just football and soccer, and 5 students played all three sports, how many students played just one sport?

Use the Venn diagram to solve the problem.

Basketball

Soccer

Football

Editing the CD to Differentiate Instruction

Creating Shortened or Tiered Tasks

While many students are able to move from one task to another, some students benefit from focusing on one task at a time. By simply separating parts of a task, either by cutting the page into sections or by using the editable CD feature to put the parts of the task on separate pages, teachers can help focus students on the first part of the task before moving them on to the next part.

In the next sample, in which all the parts of the task initially appeared in one problem together, the different parts of the task are separated. Note that the spaces for student work and the lines for writing responses were widened for students who needed more space or larger lines for writing their responses.

First Version

First Version

Name: _____

Bowl of Cherries

In the middle of the night my dad was hungry, so he came downstairs and ate $\frac{1}{2}$ of the cherries my mother had put in a bowl. My brother then came down and ate $\frac{1}{4}$ of the remaining cherries before he went back to bed. My sister came down and, you guessed it, she ate more cherries. In fact, she ate $\frac{1}{6}$ of them. When I came down I ate only $\frac{1}{5}$ of the remaining cherries. By the time my mother came down the next morning, there were only 16 cherries remaining in the bowl. How many cherries were in the bowl to start?

Show your work.

Explain how you solved the problem. _____

_____

_____

_____

_____

_____

Second Version (page 1)

Name: _____

Bowl of Cherries

In the middle of the night my dad was hungry, so he came downstairs and ate $\frac{1}{2}$ of the cherries my mother had put in a bowl.

Show your work.

My brother then came down and ate $\frac{1}{4}$ of the remaining cherries before he went back to bed.

Show your work.

(page 2)

My sister came down and, you guessed it, she ate more cherries. In fact, she ate $\frac{1}{6}$ of them.

Show your work.

When I came down I ate only $\frac{1}{5}$ of the remaining cherries.

Show your work.

(page 3)

By the time my mother came down the next morning, there were only 16 cherries remaining in the bowl. How many cherries were in the bowl to start?

Show your work.

Explain how you solved the problem.

_____

_____

_____

_____

_____

_____

_____

_____

_____

_____

Adding some fun details can generate interest and excitement in story problems, but you might prefer to modify some problems for students with limited reading ability. Simply deleting some of the words on the editable CD will result in an easy-to-read version of the same task, as shown in the second version of the following problem.

Name _____

Field Trip

On a recent field trip, students in Mrs. Ashe's third-grade class brought drinks for lunch. The drinks were stored in coolers to keep them cold. If each of the 23 students in the class brought 1 drink and each cooler held 6 drinks, how many coolers would be needed?

Show your work.

Explain how you solved the problem.

_____

_____

_____

_____

_____

Challenge: If 5 more students attended the field trip, how many more coolers would be needed now?

_____

_____

_____

Name _____

Field Trip

On a field trip, students in Mrs. Ashe's class brought drinks for lunch. Each of the 23 students in the class brought 1 drink to put in a cooler. Each cooler held 6 drinks. How many coolers would be needed?

_____

Show your work.

Explain how you solved the problem.

_____

_____

_____

_____

_____

Challenge: If 5 more students attended the field trip, how many more coolers would be needed now?

_____

_____

_____

Modifying Data

While all students may work on the same problem task, modifying the problem data will allow teachers to create varying versions of the task. Using the editable CD, you can either simplify the data or insert more challenging data including larger numbers, fractions, decimals, or percents.

Name _____

Punch Bowl

A recipe calls for 1 pint of apple juice, 3 pints of cranberry juice, and 2 quarts of ginger ale. How much punch does the recipe make?

_____

Show your work.

Explain how you determined your answer.

_____
_____
_____
_____
_____
_____
_____

Challenge: If you wanted to pour the punch into quart jars, how many jars would you need?

_____
_____
_____

Name _____

Punch Bowl

A recipe calls for $1\frac{1}{2}$ pints of apple juice, $3\frac{1}{2}$ pints of cranberry juice, and $2\frac{1}{4}$ quarts of ginger ale. How much punch does the recipe make?

_____

Show your work.

Explain how you determined your answer.

_____
_____
_____
_____
_____
_____
_____

Challenge: If you wanted to pour the punch into quart jars, how many jars would you need?

_____
_____